Bass Taverns have a proud record of serving the Liverpool public and are pleased to be associated with Freddy O'Connor's fascinating account of the role the public house has played in Liverpool's illustrious history.

© Freddy O'Connor 1995

Published by
The Bluecoat Press
Bluecoat Chambers
Liverpool
L1 3BX

ISBN 1 872568 22 X

Design: Pencilpoint
Origination: Oriel Studios
Print: Stanley Printing Company

A Pub On Every Corner

Volume One: The City Centre

Freddy O'Connor

THE BLUECOAT PRESS

Introduction

RECENTLY I read an article in a local newspaper about a tourist who had just arrived in Liverpool. After visiting the main attractions of the town, he decided to sample some of the local pubs. It did not mention which pubs he actually went into but the article went on to tell of his surprise at the high number of pubs in Liverpool.

On reading the article I smiled and thought how surprised he would have been had he visited Liverpool in the 1960s or even more astounded had he arrived a few decades earlier, when pubs were even more abundant throughout Liverpool's older areas - almost one on every corner! Of course, tourism was practically unknown then, the pubs catering mainly for the local population.

The sheer volume of pubs that thrived throughout the town was phenomenal, even within the living memory of the older generation of readers. Citizens presently aged over seventy will remember numerous pubs long since gone. I am in my mid-40s and can recall many pubs that people in their 20s and 30s would not know existed.

Therefore, in this publication I am endeavouring not only to recollect pubs within living memory, remembered with affection by those who once leant upon long gone bars, but also of forgotten hostelries wherein time was finally called many years ago. Even those readers with some knowledge of local pubs would be amazed to know how many once traded throughout Liverpool, so many that it would be an impossible task to list every one that existed. The premises that I do describe are taken from lists made before the First World War and also in the 1960s.

Ever since the first large scale demolition took place in the 1780s, Liverpool has been in a state of continual change

A typical beer house of the town so common during the 19th century and the first half of the 20th century. It stood in a most squalid area of the town at 16 Adlington Street, close to Byrom Street, with an adjoining court listed as 20 Court. Before closure in 1905, it was named Irish Man's House and managed by Bridget Gallagher.

and, sadly, little remains of ancient Liverpool. The growth of the town during the 19th century was gargantuan and thankfully we still have many fine buildings from that period. Wealth generated during the last century resulted in Liverpool having more millionaires than any other city in the country apart from London. At the other end of the social ladder, the city also amassed poorer and more squalid living conditions for the working class than anywhere else in the country.

Throughout the poverty stricken 'inner' wards of the city, disease, crime and violence were rife and the only means of escape from the tedium of life was the pub. It was common during the last century for court dwellings to have an entrance right into a public house at a time when the poor occupants of such courts would rarely venture beyond their immediate vicinity. If they were fortunate enough to come into a 'few bob' you can be sure it would go no further than the nearest pub. The fact that little other organised entertainment or recreation was available to these people was reflected in the huge number of drinking dens.

Public houses, therefore, were part and parcel of the town's development and, as grand civic buildings were erected in the city centre, many pubs also grew in stature from tiny, one-roomed beer houses to flourishing, flamboyant gin palaces. The pinnacle of the trade came during the 1890s and the years after the turn of the century. It was after this period that the phenomenal number of pubs began steadily to decline - a trend which still continues.

The demand for drinking establishments had grown rapidly towards the end of the 18th century. Many of the public houses at that time had simply been converted from dwelling houses where one or two rooms would have been converted to a 'pub', creating the slang phrase 'ale house', still used today. They were extremely bare, meagre establishments and it has been surmised that towards the close of the 18th century nearly one in seven houses sold beer.

In 1793, there were about 8,400 such outlets throughout the town with upwards of 2,000 having licences. There being such myriad establishments, the ones that were listed were often unnamed public houses, simply catalogued as PH. Also abundant were spirit vaults (SV), and wine and spirit vaults (WSV), all found in ever growing numbers, particularly throughout the poorer parts of the town (maps of Liverpool, particularly pre-1850, listed numerous pubs simply as SV even if they were named). Other abbreviations used are WSM referring to wine & spirit merchants and WSD referring to wine & spirit dealers.

In the overcrowded slum districts of Liverpool, conditions within the drinking dens of the early 19th century are difficult to comprehend today. Sanitation was primitive and men would often urinate into the spittoons which had a gully leading out into the street. Pubs would be packed day and night largely with illiterate people, where the stench and abominable conditions together with frequent drunken brawls would be an integral part of life for the inhabitants from the surrounding courts. At closing times drunken, senseless men would 'fall' out of the dimly lit pubs into the total darkness of the adjoining streets and somehow, with their built-in sense of navigation, would find their way back to their hovels. Drunkenness was for many the only escape from the dangers of a life style that was a combination of crime and vice and the ever lurking threat of death caused by the many contagious diseases associated with slum life.

As the 19th century progressed, the number of established licensed houses in the town suddenly and dramatically swelled due to an Act passed by Parliament in 1830 when, for the price of two guineas, any rate payer could apply for a licence for a beer house, resulting in some 800 being taken out in just three months.

Some of these old beer houses were the forerunners of today's off licences and, for the purpose of this publication, I shall refer to them as BH, irrespective of the different licences. From this period PHs, BHs, SVs and WSVs, flourished on an unprecedented scale, as did the building of insanitary slum property. The arrival of destitute Irish immigrants in the 1840s fleeing from the Irish potato famine caused even greater overcrowding and even more squalid living conditions. As far as licensed premises were concerned, the 'open house' situation somehow had to be curtailed, although it was not until 1869 that the issue of licences was first controlled by the Justices. Shortly after this, in 1872, pubs were forced to close at 11 p.m.

Despite the struggle to control the number of licensed premises, by the 1860s over 3,000 were flourishing in the town. One estimate from that period reckoned that over £70,000 was taken over the counters daily! A truly staggering amount considering the abject poverty of the time. The figure of over 3,000 included clubs which, at that time, were not under police control, opening and closing whenever they liked. In 1865, the number of licensed premises, excluding clubs, was still 2,841. Many of these premises were not pubs as we know them today, often they were entered through shops, such as grocers or tobacconists, into dismal drinking dens and in many cases (an impossible number to estimate), would not have been licensed.

Castle Street, for instance, is among the finest streets of the town containing splendid Victorian buildings. However, during the last century, prior to these magnificent offices being built, a number of pubs that could only be reached through shop fronts stood in the street, in some cases having entrances in Lower Castle Street.

British Workman Public House Co. Ltd. This company, an offshoot of the temperance movement, was established in 1875. Although sounding like a public house the premises did not sell intoxicating liquor. The object of the company was as follows: 'A place where working men could find the warmth, advantages and attractions of a public house without intoxicating drink being sold, but where tea, coffee, cocoa and other wholesome refreshments could be obtained for a small charge'.

The large number of public houses in 19th-century Liverpool, although for so long overlooked by the authorities, was not totally ignored. During the 1830s, other towns throughout the country, like Liverpool, were plagued with drunkenness. It was in Preston, in 1833, that the 'Temperance Society' was founded. It was a society totally opposed to drink, which soon grew in strength countrywide and was a force to be reckoned with, eventually encouraging the government to enforce public houses to introduce fixed hours and instigating the ban on children being served.

Cocoa rooms and Liverpool Public House Co. Ltd (despite the name no alcohol was sold on these premises) had been founded in 1875 during a nine-week religious campaign conducted in Liverpool in February and March of that year by two American Evangelists, Sankey and Moody. Some Liverpool Christian businessmen pooled their resources to erect a huge wooden structure, Victoria Hall, Victoria Street with a capacity for approximately 8,000 people. Services were held three times a day and were packed to overflowing. The following article is from a former weekly paper, *The Porcupine*:

'Three weeks have passed ... And still may be seen the eager crowds hurrying towards Victoria Hall in thousands. What means it? Why come they? What hear they? ... From aristocratic Aigburth, Woolton and the South End come the refined and intelligent, high and the low churchgoers: Everton, Kirkdale and Bootle send their middle classes, composed chiefly of methodists and presbyterians: but the benighted districts of Scotland Road, Vauxhall Road and adjacent streets obey not the "call", and few fustian jackets and bonnetless women mingle in the throng which three times daily passes along Victoria Street ... From almost every village and town of Lancashire and Cheshire come the wicked and the good. Even religion - loving Wales is offering its devotion at the shrine of the great revivalists.'

Like the Temperance Movement, preachers were committed to converting the public to religion from public houses; they never quite achieved their aim, although by 1903 some 65 alcohol free establishments were in existence. By the 1920s, the religious beginnings were forgotten and the name was changed to the Liverpool City Caterers, still trading in the 1970s but by then reduced to a handful of 'canteens' around the Dock Road area.

Many 'temperance' hotels opened up throughout the city centre where alcohol would not be allowed on the premises. For example, several were listed in Mount Pleasant, all of which eventually turned into conventional

NUMBER 11 COURT, Burlington Street (1934)
Faced by such depressing living conditions, it is no wonder the public house became the social hub of the local community.

hotels. Similarly, the hotels which still line Lord Nelson Street were also temperance hotels during the last century. Ironically, in March 1993, the government announced children would be allowed into pubs; an issue that has turned full circle. It was in 1908 that children under the age of fourteen were banned from public houses to discourage street urchins from going into them to beg for coppers or to buy 'jugs out' for their parents. Today, the government's intention is to create a more family style of public house.

A number of court entrances are featured alongside public houses in the photographs in this book. For readers not familiar with courts, they were the unsanitary dwellings for thousands of poor and destitute citizens of the city's slums. After 1840, one toilet and one tap were installed to serve an average of 30 families. Daylight and fresh air were unknown in the early courts until the 1860s when they were given 'open' entrances. Previous to this, many courts were entered through an opening only two feet wide and 20 feet or longer in length. Little wonder disease was abundant during the 19th century. The last of the city's court dwellings were cleared by the 1960s.

In common with these hovels, pubs built prior to 1830 also had no means of sanitation, and the conditions people endured would be difficult to visualise today. When sewers were laid out throughout the town it solved some of the problems. However, like housing, pubs were also slow to make improvements and older readers may still remember when pubs had urinal stones located outside (thereafter progressing to 'Gents' toilets, usually in the yard of a pub. Many still exist throughout the city today, although now covered over and completely modernised). Ladies toilets, taken for granted nowadays, were unknown. Numerous

public men's toilets once stood in Liverpool's main streets and would often be outside public houses from the days when the pubs may not have had their own.

Many people who frequented pubs did not know the names of the establishments yet all would know their nicknames, this being a legacy from the days when most pubs actually had no name and, therefore, a nickname would have been adopted. Many nicknames were taken from managers' or former managers' names. Others may have been due to the pub's location or to some significant remark or incident that may have occurred and somehow stuck.

For example, the Foot Hospital on Scotland Road (formerly the Grapes) has now adopted its former nickname as the pub's name. I was informed the reason for this name derived from a customer who, having had too much to drink, fell over the step of the pub and, on falling shouted, 'Me foot's gone, take me to the foot hospital' (or words to that effect!). This simple, instant remark was immediately associated with the pub and, once given, a nickname would stick (this story may well be true, as a foot hospital did exist in Liverpool). Over generations, even when pubs were eventually named, many of the old nicknames would stick, this still being true today. In fact, a recent trend is to rename pubs with their old nicknames.

The fall in the number of pubs in the town centre and immediate areas dramatically increased with war damage and the large demolition programmes which took place after the war, causing a massive shift in population from those areas. Previously, the 1930s had seen the creation of the new 'garden' estates, notably the Speke and Norris Green areas, where people were rehoused from the central districts. The building of tenement 'garden' blocks was also a huge improvement on previous conditions. Gerard Gardens, for example, replaced the former slum ridden Gerard Street and vicinity and St Andrews Gardens replaced the squalid St Andrew Street locality. Although these and many similar blocks of flats were constructed to replace slums, by the 1960s they too were classed as unfit and the majority of them have now been demolished. New housing estates, however, built away from the central areas had amenities such as gardens, bathrooms, hot and cold water etc., which were all vast improvements on the previous quality of life. Yet, for all the improvements, the people were no different and for many of the residents one factor was lost forever: the short stroll to the local. The large Norris Green estate, for example, did not have one single pub built on it. It was not surprising, therefore, that four pubs skirting the estate: the Crown, Western Approaches, Royal Oak and the Broadway were among the busiest in Liverpool.

The post-war demolition programme resulted in the population moving further and further away from the

GRAPES (FOOT HOSPITAL)
A Threlfalls house managed by Herbert Maguire when photographed in the 1950s. It has opened and closed on a number of occasions over the past few years. Listed as 291 Scotland Road at the junction of Silvester Street. The shops viewed were previously listed as: 289 John Girvan, Chemist & Druggist; 287 William G. Taffe (Surgery) M.B., C.H.B.; 285 Mrs Gladys Niven, Confectioner. Together with the pub they are all presently closed.

town, causing drinkers to become more and more isolated and distant from their former locals. Many still travelled into town by car or public transport but with the ever increasing cost and, in the case of the motorist, the Law's stance to combat the menace of drink driving, many drinkers gave up travelling into town altogether and instead settled for their new locals in the many estates away from the town centre. While some former 'townies' would venture into the centre on the odd occasion or weekends, only a few would regularly visit the city centre. Town at the weekend, as always, is a flourish of activity in the pubs and clubs, particularly with younger people, but through the week it is only a shadow of former days when the local population lived just a stone's throw away. Nowadays many of the city centre pubs close on various midweek days, some even closing on Sunday evenings.

Social changes from the 1960s onwards altered drinking habits enormously. The life style of the working class changed more than in any other previous decade. Many people took holidays abroad, which were virtually unknown and considered a luxury in the austerity years of the late '40s and early '50s. Fashion changed more than ever before, whilst cars, televisions, washing machines etc. all became within the reach of the working class. In pubs, juke boxes began to replace the piano and sing-a-long.

Drinking habits also changed, particularly the promotion of lager. Interestingly, lager had been brewed in this country since the 1880s and a short lived brewery named the British Lager Brewery Co. Ltd existed in Devon Street between 1899 and 1902. Outside of Britain, 95 per cent of the world drank lager or lager related drinks. But lager, although available, was not very popular; as far as many were concerned it was a 'woman's drink' and no self-respecting male would drink it! It was not until the late 1960s that lager became popular with male drinkers, coinciding with the massive television advertising campaigns. Lager sales now account for half the UK beer market. Nowadays, a wide variety of lagers is available, although still frowned upon by traditional beer drinkers. (The majority of lagers sold in this country and bearing foreign sounding 'brand' names are in fact brewed here.)

In recent years, 'wine bars', licensed cafes and European-style eating/drinking establishments together with recently constructed pubs are becoming a regular feature of the city centre. Being a comparatively new concept they are not within the scope of this book and are therefore omitted, unless relevant to a particular pub or building.

Within the last few years, beer prices have escalated on an unprecedented scale. Just a few years ago pubs were thriving throughout the week when people had the money to go out for a few pints. A tradition now all but dead is when a person, generally employed in the forces, after being away from home would walk into their local and buy a 'round' for everyone in the pub. This of course mainly occurred during the war and post-war years when drinking was the norm for thousands of men in all types of work. Similarly, the days where relatives would drink in the same pub have diminished, a tradition that faded with the destruction of the old communities when families were scattered everywhere. These changes in social habits have changed the nature of pubs. Their future survival will depend on their ability to adapt to new trends in eating and drinking, which are moving closer to a continental style of life.

PHILHARMONIC HOTEL
As Liverpool's wealth grew, pubs also flourished. The Philharmonic, on Hope Street, is perhaps the most famous example of the flamboyant gin palaces of the turn-of-the-century years.

A Pub On Every Corner

The 1875 map showing licensed premises within 200 yards of the Town Hall perfectly illustrates the title of this book. I have added my own comments to the original text.

1 William Child, 21 Harrington Street, the Harrington Restaurant - these licensed premises can be entered from three doorways in Pekin Court. [Later and presently New Crocodile (19)]

2 J.A. Roberts, 4 Harrington Street (Wason Buildings), Wine Rooms - no name over the door, as required by Act of Parliament. [Later named the Clarence Wine Bar]

3 Edward Spencer, 14 Cook Street (Law Association Rooms), Luncheon Rooms. [Site presently two licensed houses, Dempsey's and City Vaults]

4 John Munslow, 19 North John Street, Old House At Home. [4 & 5: This is the Solicitors Law Stationary Society Building built in 1854, as stated on the map was the Old House At Home during the 1870s. Prior to that date a PH named the Yorkshire House stood on this site adjoining another named Caernarvon Castle, later Melbourne Hotel (5 on map). The facade was reconstructed in 1975, it now has Melbourne Buildings written on it]

5 John Jackson, 17 North John Street, Melbourne Hotel - this house goes through into Princes Street, with an entrance in that street.

6 Elizabeth Wilde, 5 Temple Lane, Restaurant.

7 John Hall, 24 Dale Street, (Temple) Restaurant - later Temple Bar. [Appears to be in the wrong location, although behind the Temple the premises may have extended that far]

8 Robert C. Gardner, 34 Dale Street (Colonial Buildings), WSM. [This was to become the town's first Yates's Wine Lodge some fifteen years later]

9 Robert Saker, 22 Dale Street, Angel Hotel and Angel Vaults - the Angel Hotel and Angel Vaults at the corner of North John Street, both under one licence, but the tenant's name up in two places. A.B. Walker's name figures at this establishment.

10 Peter Craig, 6 North John Street, Oyster Rooms

11 Thomas P. Manders, 16 North John Street (Union Building), WSM.

12 Charles Luker, 1 Union Court, Restaurant and WSM.

13 William Fisk, 25 Castle Street, Cook And Confectioner - house closed, no application for renewal.

14 Joseph Fairhurst, 13-15 Castle Street, Restaurant, Swifts Court.

15 Alice Buchanan, 11a Castle Street (Swift Court), Dean Swift's Snuff Box.

16 Alfred W. Marshall, 9 Castle Street (Taylor's Shop) - licence not taken up.

17 5a Castle Street (Slater Court), Restaurant and WSM.

18 Martha E. Rigby, 6 Dale Street, Wine & Spirit Dealers - no ownership returned in the police register when examined.

19 Robert Fair, 12 Dale Street, WSM.

20 Albert W. Sims, 18 Dale Street, Stock Exchange Chambers, Restaurant.

21 Frederick Butters, 14 Dale Street (York Buildings), WSD & Restaurant - with an entrance in Sweeting Street. [This also appears to be in the wrong location, although it does state having an entrance in Sweeting Street. By the 1890s this was named the Queens Buffet]

22 Francis Kenrick, 8 Sweeting Street, Old House At Home - known as the bus driver's hotel.

23 William Mossop Keen, 16-18 Castle Street, Cigar And Wine Merchant, Hineson's Tobacco Shop - there is no appearance of a public house in Castle Street, you enter through a passage in Lower Castle Street.

24 Charlotte Kynaston, 17 Lower Castle Street, Refreshment Rooms 'The Arch' - though licensed for Lower Castle Street has an entrance from Castle Street.

25 James Harrop, 4 Brunswick Street, WSM.

26 James Harris, 15 Lower Castle Street, Restaurant.

27 S.S. Carpenter, 11 Lower Castle Street, WSM, licence revoked.

28 Robert Slatters, 6 Lower Castle Street, Wine Merchants.

29 Robert Bennett, 17 Fenwick Street, WSM - this house has an entrance in Lower Castle Street.

30 William Spencer, 17a Fenwick Street, Restaurant.

31 Nathan Morrell, 19 Fenwick Street, the London - this house has entrances from Fenwick Street, Moor Street and Lower Castle Street.

32 William Airey, 3-5 Lower Castle Street, Coach And Horses.

33 Jane Child, 39-41 Lower Castle Street, Restaurant. [Listed in the 1890s as the Alliance Hotel and closed in 1901. The premises added to the North & South Wales Branch Bank]

34 Thomas Chapman, 5 Moor Street, British And Foreign Wine Dealer - the principal entrance to this house appears to be 10 James Street.

35 Elizabeth Hannah, 6 Moor Street, the Bulls Head And Dining Rooms.

36 Leigh Lyons, 5 Old Ropery, Corn Exchange Tavern.

37 Amos Stevenson, 1 Old Ropery, Corn Market Hotel. [Corn Exchange Tavern open to date. On the map listed as Corn Market Hotel, whilst

35 is listed as Bulls Head And Dining Rooms in parallel Moor Street. Both premises are now one and named the Corn Market after the former Corn Exchange built in Brunswick Street in 1851. Two more PH's, the Corn Exchange Tavern and another Corn Market Hotel are shown on the map in this vicinity and have since been cleared]

38 Richard Airey, 22 Drury Lane, Liverpool Arms.

39 Hugh Green, 7 Brunswick Street (Brunswick Buildings), WSM.

40 Richard Coate, 14-16 Drury Lane, the Corn Market Hotel.

41 Mary Hughes, 13a Drury Lane (Middleton Chambers), Restaurant.

42 Emily Munroe, 9 Drury Lane, Old Mansion House Hotel.

43 Mary Ann Brick, Brunswick Street (India Buildings), Atlantic Newsrooms

44 Helen Reardon, 15 Water Street, Restaurant. [Later named the Arches having a side door which led into Canton Buildings]

45 Frank Cox, 25 Water Street, Restaurant.

46 Frederick Roberts, Water Street (Tower Buildings) Luncheon Rooms.

47 Sarah Cunningham, 1 Old Church Yard, Old Stile House.

48 Ferdinand Rothwell, 16 Water Street (Oriel Close), Restaurant.

49 Margaret Allday, 12 Covent Garden, Pig And Whistle.

50 William Bennett, 5 Chapel Street, Dining And Luncheon Rooms.

51 Liverpool Limited Wine Cellar, Exchange - no victualler listed.

52 Arthur Ballard (Exchange Passage West), Exchange Buildings, Liverpool Dining Rooms.

53 George L. Baker, 2 Rumford Street, BH.

54 Thomas Vincent, 4 Chapel Street (Adelaide Buildings) Wine Merchant.

55 Thomas Williams, 14 Chapel Street, Manchester Arms. [Later named Manchester And Bolton PH]

56 Catherine Williams, Chapel Street (Exchange Alley) Luncheon Rooms. [This appears to be in the wrong position, an alley named Exchange Alley North existed behind Adelaide Buildings which was a little north of 54 on the map. In this alley was a PH named the Alexandra Shades]

57 Thomas Ashburner and George L. Baker, 1 Rumford Place, Wine Merchants.

58 Raymond Darlington, 20 Chapel Street, WSM. [This was later named the Manchester Arms and the following is from a 1892 police report: 'The licensed premises are in the basement of the building. There is a door which opens from the yard into a large building at the rear leading to Rumford Place in which there are a number of offices. The sanitary conveniences in the yard are used in common by the occupiers of both premises.']

59 Henry Gill, 34 Chapel Street, Lancelot's Vaults.

60 Charles Owen, 36 Fazakerley Street, Pilot Boat Inn.

61 Margaret Owen, 34 Fazakerley Street, BH. [The writing preceding this PH on the list obviously not applying by 1903 as the following police report was for 34 by then named the Pilot Boat: 'This house is registered as a common lodging house and is in a very dilapidated condition.']

62 Thomas Morgan, 30 Fazakerley Street, BH.

63 Margaret Davies, 20 Fazakerley Street, BH. [Later named Beaumaris Tavern. Another pub of Fazakerley Street was listed as 2 (& 25 Old Hall Street) Exchange Vaults, earlier Fleece]

64 John Main, Old Hall Street (1 Central Court), The Albany.

65 Elizabeth Sowerby, 2 Old Hall Street, Restaurant. [From the 1880s named the Exchange Oyster Stores then from the 1920s known as Boyle's after the proprietress at that time. Rebuilt building containing a bar presently named Sam's]

66 William Harding, Tithebarn Street (Liver Chambers), Restaurant. [Later United Powers PH]

67 John Seagrave, Tithebarn Street (Northern Assurance Chambers), WSM.

68 John B. Buckley, 60 Tithebarn Street (Knowsley Building), WSV. [Appears to be the wrong number, should be 15]

69 Robert Arden, 10 Key Street, Travellers Rest.

70 Mary Morrish, Tithebarn Street Station Restaurant (Railway Arches).

71 William Leatherbarrow, 30 Tithebarn Street, Green Doors PH. [Central PH]

72 Henry Edmondson, 28 Tithebarn Street, Lion Tavern.

73 Henry Moore, 26 Tithebarn Street, Refreshment Rooms. [Later incorporated into the Lion PH]

74 Thomas Gardner, 20a Tithebarn Street, Railway Inn.

75 Thomas Twiss, 3 Tempest Hey, Beer Cellar.

76 William H. Beckett, Moorfields (Leith Offices), Wine Merchants.

77 William Bilsborough, 41 Moorfields, listed 43-45 Cross Keys. [This PH, Cross Keys, became one of Yates's Wine Lodges during the 1890s, still there today, as one of only two left in the city centre, although it was rebuilt after war damage. In 1899 the manager, H. Gronan, was fined 2/6d with 2/6d costs for 'Refusing to receive two soldiers billeted upon him.']

78 William J. Gillies, 15-17 Tempest Hey, Globe Vaults. [Later named the Waterloo]

79 Alfred T. Lowe, 6 Tempest Hey, WSM.

80 Julius Franks, 30 Exchange Street East (Mellors Buildings), Wine And Brandy Merchant.

81 John B. Maycock, 28 Exchange Street East (Masons Buildings), WSV.

82 David Anderson, 26 Exchange Street East (Exchange Court) Luncheon Rooms. [Listed as a Luncheon Rooms yet its name, Crooked Billet, has been listed on this site since the 18th century. The building goes through to Hackin's Hey where this section has been in use as a night club for many years]

83 Henry Bird, 24 Exchange Street East, Luncheon Bar.

84 Richard Anderson, 22 Exchange Street East, Restaurant. [Later Bull & Bear]

85 Charles Baker, 4 Exchange Street East, WSD.

86 John Hughes, 15 Hackins Hey, Conway Castle.

87 Mary Ferries, 5 Hackins Hey, Dining Rooms. [Later Peacock Buffet]

88 John Dwyer Allen, 1 Dale Street (Queen Buildings), WSM. [Appears to be incorrectly listed, as 1 Dale Street is the site of the Bank of Scotland which is mentioned next but one. This site on the map is the Union Marine Building on whose ground floor stood the Bodega PH, earlier George Hotel before that Cross Keys Hotel]

89 John Taylor, 13-15 Dale Street, Palatine Hotel.

90 Thomas Gillow, 2-6 Hackins Hey, WSM. [Strange this is not named and was listed as WSM, 2-6 Hackins Hey. This is the Hole In The Wall 2-4]

91 Bridget Malone, 8 Hackins Hey, Dining Rooms.

92 William Naylor, 10 Hackins Hey, Denbigh Castle.

93 James Purvis, 23-25 Dale Street, Wine & Brandy Merchant.

94 Thomas Keyt, 23 Tempest Hey, Restaurant.

95 Edward W. Tomlin, 29 Dale Street, Billiard Rooms.

96 Henry N. Abbinett, 31 Dale Street, George Hotel. [This was earlier the site of the Wellington Hotel and from 1880 was listed as the Reform Club Buildings]

97 Henry G. Kewney, 5 Exchange Street East (Liverpool & London Chambers) WSM. [97 & 98 Listed as Liverpool & London Chambers (1855-1857). This was the site of the town's first Town Hall, now the Bank of Scotland, 1 Dale Street]

98 Sarah Bell, 5 Exchange Street East (Liverpool & London Chambers) Restaurant.

99 William O. Candeland, 43 Dale Street, City Arms.

Brewing and Breweries

Brewing is an ancient trade. It is known that the Egyptians of 5,000 years ago were skilled brewers and habitual beer drinkers. The Romans, after their conquest of England, built roadside refreshment houses known as 'Tabernae Diversorae'. At such 'tabernae' or as they were also known, 'tavernae', a night's lodging could be found. These were the forerunners of the country's taverns.

Such establishments were crudely swept away after the Anglo-Saxon invasion and it was left to the monasteries to continue the art of brewing. Over the centuries, as travel became more common, monasteries found their guest chambers insufficient for demand and had to extend parts of the monasteries into separate 'lodging houses', which eventually became 'inns'. Eventually, both inns and taverns were numerous throughout the country and many of the ancient establishments thrive today. Two surviving near Liverpool are the Punch Bowl and Scotch Piper Inn.

The Punch Bowl, located in Sefton, is reputed to have once been the school house of the adjoining Sefton Parish Church which dates back to the 11th century. The Scotch Piper Inn, located in Lydiate, dates back to c.1320 and is possibly the oldest inn of Lancashire. Originally called the Royal Oak, its name changed around the 1740s during the Jacobite Rebellion. The reason for this was a battle in the vicinity in which a Scottish Piper was injured. The innkeeper's daughter, after hiding him, nursed him back to good health and eventually married him; the inn was henceforth called the Scotch Piper.

The term 'ale' supposedly originated from the Danish invasion, is derived from the Danish word 'ol' (the word 'beer' is Anglo-Saxon and was probably used synonymously with the word 'ale' for centuries). Ale, or beer as we know it today, stems from the introduction of hops, which are thought to have been brought to this country by a Kent merchant about 1520. Typical of the British even then, change was frowned upon and it took a long time for hops to be accepted. Generally speaking, after the introduction of hops, the term 'beer' was used for 'hopped' beer with the term 'ale' used for the lighter-coloured beers. By the end of the 18th century, all varieties of beers were 'hopped' and the words of ale and beer were henceforth used for any beer or stout. Hops are grown throughout Kent and Sussex and, before the First World War, thousands of mainly poor people from the London area travelled to Kent to 'pick the hops'. In 1908, 100,000 workers and their families descended on the south-east. By the Second World War, 60 special trains commuted to the south-east and it was not until 1960 trains stopped bringing workers to pick hops, mechanisation finally ending what was for most of them their only holiday, albeit a working one.

The first known recorded brewer in Liverpool was William Furnival who resided in Water Street around 1680. The first known purpose built brewery in the town was in Dale Street under the ownership of James Blair and was in production between 1787 and 1793. Prior to this date, breweries did exist but would have been small, insignificant establishments behind inns and taverns.

From the late 18th century, breweries grew throughout Liverpool at an unprecedented rate to over 40 in operation by the 1790s. (Nationally, by 1900, over 6,000 brewers existed although by the outbreak of the Second World War there were less than 600.) The largest in Liverpool was

Porter's brewery in Scotland Place, opened in 1794 by Joshua Rose, a local merchant and landowner. It claimed it produced as good a quality of liquor as the London brewers. Porter's Ale was first brewed in London around 1722, and lays claim to being the nation's first popular beer. The name seemingly originated from the London porters working in the markets.

As more and more beers came on the market, the old 'porter' ale eventually became obsolete; it was last brewed in Dublin in 1973.

'Stout' was a name originally given to a porter of extra strength. The world renowned Guinness brewers are famous for their stout which is still available in most licensed premises. So established is the name, it is not bought as a 'pint of stout' but a 'pint of Guinness' (during the 1840s there was a brewery in the Goree named Guinness & Co., but is doubtful they were related to the more famous family).

The city centre and older parts of the town also contained numerous breweries during the last century. A prime example is one of the original streets of the town - Dale Street. The frontage of Dale Street presently houses some of Liverpool's splendid architecture including Queen Insurance Buildings (1839), Municipal Buildings (1860-66), the Temple (1864-65), Municipal Annex (1883), Royal Insurance Buildings (1897-1903) and State Insurance Building (1906). The construction of these buildings replaced just a few of the many pubs and breweries which existed on Dale Street. The following is a list of brewers that once lined Dale Street, though probably more existed than those shown. Today, it contains only a handful of pubs and not a single brewery.

William Atkinson	1804-05	James Blair	1787-93
Thomas Brandreth	1790s	James Chorley	1790s
Dale & Co.	1780s	Daniel Daulby	1787-89
Daulby & Crook	1767-69	Caryl Fleetwood	1760s
Robert Gortside	1790s	William Harvey	1780s
James Johnson	1780s	John Johnson	1781-1803
Joseph Johnson	1804-1810	Richard Johnson	1787-1810
Mark Lawrence	1790s	Robert Lawrence	1766-1783
Robert Lawrence	1790s	Marshall & Brown	1816-1824
Thomas Ogle	1820s	George Ormerod	1760s
Thomas Percival	1790s	James Petty	1810
Thomas Pinlow	1770s	Randles & Walker	1796-1814
Shuttleworth & Co.	1767	Sleeman & Co.	1860s
Edward Tatlock	1767-72	John Thomson	1813-14
John Thomson	1816	Walker Randles	1860s
Joseph Walker	1796-1814	Daniel Webster	1860s
Ellen Whythell	1770s	John Widnall	1840s
Ralph Williams	1760s	Ann Wyatt	1766-74

To put some perspective to this list, it can be assumed that with the majority being short lived, they were mainly inferior brewers-cum-drinking establishments on the same premises, the forerunner of the public/beer houses described shortly.

The dates of the opening of these breweries were not coincidental but were linked with the town's development. In 1700, there were no docks, only an open harbour; manufacturing was practically non-existent and there was only one church for worshippers. The town's revenue in 1699 was £804 4s 3d, and the population less than 6,000. By 1800, there were five floating docks which, together with dry docks and basins, contained 26 acres. Manufacturing included brewing, ship-building, several mills, sugar houses, iron founders, tobacco and snuff manufacturers, glass works and watch making. There were thirteen churches, the town's revenue had increased to £82,393 17s 9d and the population had expanded to over 80,000.

Over the years, the small brewers gradually began to diminish due to closure, amalgamations and takeovers. By the 1920s the following existed in Liverpool:

P. Walker & Sons Ltd: PHs 382, BHs 29, total 411.
P. Walker (Warrington, & R. Cain & Sons): PHs 244, BHs 3, total 247.
Higsons: PHs 116, BHs 13, total 129.

CONWAY ARMS
Conway Street, nicknamed the 'Flat Iron', possibly after the famous building in Chicago. Birkenhead was an important centre of the brewing trade.

Bents: PHs 120, BHs 7, total 127.

Threlfalls: PHs 124, BH 1, total 125.

Robinsons: Formerly of Holly Street, taken over by Ind Coope in 1920 who owned PHs 39, BHs 2, total 41.

Greenall Whitley: Although a Warrington brewery, a member of this family, Edward Greenall, had a brewery in Cunliffe Street, off Tithebarn Street, as long ago as 1788, moving to Vauxhall Road in the early 19th century.

PHs 35, BHs 5, total 40 (in Liverpool).

Mellors (see Walker/Cain): PHs 31, total 31.

Bramleys: Formerly of Upper Hill Street, taken over by Hope & Anchor brewery of Sheffield in 1948.

PHs 17, total 17.

Ind Coope: Later part of Allied Breweries Ltd.

PHs 16, total 16.

Houldings: Formerly of Tynemouth Street, Everton, taken over by Ind Coope in 1938. PHs 14, total 14.

Smarts: Formerly of Chaucer Street, off Scotland Road, taken over by Walkers in 1937. PHs 13, total 13.

Yates Castle Brewery Limited: A Birkenhead brewery with a number of outlets in Liverpool. Williams Yates was a Manchester brewer who formed a partnership with Charles Gatehouse of Birkenhead and brewed at the Castle Brewery, Ardwick, Manchester. Yates also owned another company named William Yates & Co. Brewers, whilst Charles Gatehouse also had his own separate business established in Cleveland Street, Birkenhead (formerly Aspinall's Brewery who in 1865 merged with Cooks Brewery of Oxton Road to eventually form the Birkenhead Brewery Co. Limited). This brewery merged with Threlfalls in 1962 with 120 licensed houses.

WILBRAHAM HOTEL
Listed as 23 Wilbraham Street, off Scotland Road, at the junction of Oswald Street. A typical Bents corner local. Photographed in the early 1970s before demolition, the manageress was Kathleen McCormack. 'King Hal', not the name of the pub but a popular beer advertisement featured on many Bents establishments.

ST PAUL'S HOTEL
Listed as 16 Earl Street at the junction of St Paul's Square, it is one of the few old structures still standing hereabouts. Photographed in the early 1960s with the almost completed huge J.M. Centre looming in the background. During the last century this pub was named the Vine Tavern; it is closed at the time of writing.

In 1888 William Yates bought out his partner. Gatehouse and Son later formed another brewery in Birkenhead, the West Cheshire Brewery Company Limited in 1896, at the Queens Brewery, Farm Road, Tranmere. This was also taken over by Threlfalls in 1927 with 67 licensed houses.

Yates Castle Brewery (Birkenhead) seems to have been established in 1896 as an offshoot of William Yates and Company who had the original Castle Brewery at Ardwick. A Castle Brewery was listed to Gatehouse and Yates in Market Place, Birkenhead between 1877 and 1889. This brewery was taken over in 1961 by John Smiths.

The total number of licensed houses controlled by these breweries was 1,217 (which, together with other smaller outlets, amounted to 1,354 licensed houses in Liverpool) during the 1920s, less than a third of the total some 80 years earlier.

With the general decline of pubs and breweries only the following four major breweries existed in Liverpool by the 1960s: Bents, Higsons, Threlfalls and Walkers. At the time of writing only the latter is still trading.

BENTS

Richard Bent founded his Scotland Road brewery in 1810. He was joined by his nephew John Bent of Newcastle, Staffordshire, who, on the death of his uncle, acquired a site in Johnson Street for the brewery in 1821. Throughout the 19th century, the brewery operated in Johnson Street on various sites under the management of Bent & Lunt and Rowland Bent & Co. In 1899, Rowland Bent & Co. (126 PHs) and Montgomery of Stone,

HIGSONS BREWERY
The Stanhope Street brewery in 1989, still displaying the defunct Higsons name. Their final move was in 1923 to the former Cains Brewery in Stanhope Street, then named Mersey Bry. Here they remained as the last of Liverpool's large breweries until 1985 when they merged with Boddingtons of Manchester and closed down in 1990. This closure, the last of some 90 breweries, leaves Liverpool the only main city in the country without a major brewery (see Cains). At the time of its closure the company had about 80 PHs. A former brewery that was taken over by Higsons in 1927 was Joseph Jones & Co. (Knotty Ash) Ltd., registered in 1924 with 70 pubs previously Joseph Jones & Co. 1869-1924. The Lord Nelson public house in Prescot Road, Knotty Ash, was a former 'tap' room of the brewery.

HIGSONS
Merseyside's Famous
ALES
BREWED ON MERSEYSIDE SINCE 1780

A Higsons' advertisement with the docks used as a background.

Staffordshire (32 PHs) amalgamated to form Bents Brewery Company Limited. The company remained in Johnson Street and, in 1967, was taken over by Bass Charrington who ceased brewing there in 1975.

The final takeover bid by the Bass Charrington Company was not easy because of Bent's strong presence in Liverpool. Other brewers, including Bass, Watney Mann, Mitchell and Butler (who by the 1960s had a holding in Bents), had attempted to acquire the brewery. In fact, no large brewer during the 1960s would have ignored the opportunity to acquire Bents who, at that time, operated three breweries: Liverpool (Johnson Street), Ashton-under-Lyne (Garside Brewery) and Stone, Staffordshire.

Liverpool produced about 2,000 barrels a week, Ashton about 700 and Stone slightly less. The licensed houses situated around the three production areas consisted of approximately 200 in Liverpool, 180 in south-east Lancashire & south-west Yorkshire, 60 in Staffordshire and 80 in North Wales, Shropshire and Cheshire.

Although it is now over 20 years since Bents were taken over, the name is still frequently referred to throughout the

city and one of Bass's hardest tasks was to alter the poor image of the old Bents houses. Prior to the 1970s, drinkers and managers alike would confirm this to be true. Why Bents? One probable reason is the fact that Bents always sold the cheapest beer in Liverpool which, of course, although good for the customer also attracted the less desirable customers. Guinness, for example, was sold a ha'penny cheaper than the other breweries as Bents shipped it over in bulk direct from Dublin. They sold a remarkable 120,000 bottles of Guinness per week, rising to a staggering 240,000 during the Christmas period.

Before 1960, if you were to visit a local pub just a few miles from Liverpool, you would find various games being played in the pub's bar such as dominoes and shove-a-ha'penny and the customers' social life would revolve around such games. However, in Liverpool drinking only was the order of the day, partially due to the prejudices of the Liverpool Licensing Authorities. In the words of a former Bents director: 'The magistrates were very tough, backed up by an equally tough police force. There was no drinking after hours, no singing and dancing, no games and

1938 PARLOUR PRICES

		per small
Scotch Whisky	- -	7d.
Irish Whisky	- -	7d.
Rum and Gin	- -	7d.
Own Proprietary Spirits-		8d.
Crown·Vat Liqueur Scotch		9d.
Hollands	- -	9d.
French Brandy	-	10d.
One Star Brandy	-	11d.
Three Star Brandy	-	1/1
Port and Sherry	-	4d.
Claret	- -	4d.

Daniel Higson, Ltd., Liverpool.

1938 PARLOUR PRICES

Mild Ale	- - -	per Pint	6d.
Best Mild	- -	per Pint	8d.
Bitter Ale -	-	per Pint	8d.
Stingo	-	Half Pint	5d.
Bass Bitter	-	per Pint	9d.
Bottled Higson's Pale Ale -		per Bott.	5½d.
Bottled Bass	-	per Bott.	6d.
Bottled Guinness		per Bott.	6d.
Nips Guinness -		per Bott.	4½d.
Nips, Stingo	-	per Bott.	5d.

Daniel Higson, Ltd., Brewers, Liverpool.

Higsons parlour prices in 1938.

no darts allowed in the pubs,' (strangely, this director seems to have overlooked billiards, a game played for years in the city's pubs*).

Not surprisingly, this kind of regime encouraged a unitarian type of managed house and Bents, in common with other Liverpool breweries, tended to build large, austere houses, where the emphasis was suited to hard drinking only. This seemed to satisfy most drinkers in Liverpool, until a change of attitude gradually set into the drinking fraternity from the 1950s. As another director once said: 'Conditions and expectations were very different on Merseyside. In many pubs the most important member of the bar staff was the Alsatian.'

At the time of the old Bents takeover by Bass Charrington they had 514 PHs. Today, Bass Charrington have some 90 pubs around Liverpool (this figure is, of course, continually changing) and they are presently the largest brewers in the country with over 7,000 PHs and 13 breweries.

HIGSONS

A brewery was established in Dale Street in 1780, probably the second purpose-built one in Liverpool. It belonged to the Harvey family, who later added a further

purpose-built brewery in 1803 situated at 60 Cheapside. The family was involved in many different businesses in Liverpool and it is possible that a member of this family was the person who gave Lime Street its name from his lime-kilns that once stood there.

The brewery was run by the family until 1845 when Robert Ellison Harvey decided to sell up. Having no children he sold the business, but not the premises, to Thomas Howard who belonged to another old Liverpool family involved in brewing. Howard appointed Daniel Higson as a cashier and office manager. In 1865, Howard, then a sick man, took to the spa waters of Harrogate and it was here he passed away. Shortly before, he had revoked all previous wills and made a new one, leaving his entire personal estate and effects to Daniel Higson. The business was run by Daniel Higson for several years as executor until 1875, when it was henceforth named Daniel Higson Ltd.

By 1909, the executors only gave a three year lease to the Cheapside location as they had decided they were going to sell the property to the Post Office. Having to find new premises, the company acquired the Windsor Brewery in Upper Parliament Street and moved in during January, 1914. It was taken over the same year by Sykes Wine & Spirit Merchants but retained the name Higsons.

THRELFALLS

Like Bents, although not as well known, the name Threlfalls is still recognised throughout the city, usually as 'Threllies'. This brewery was founded in 1812 by John Threlfall and was situated at Crosbie Street (off St James Street) until it was demolished around 1860. They also obtained premises in Trueman Street off Dale Street, in 1847. In 1850, Threlfalls acquired a brewery in Salford and, in 1861, operated from Cook Street, Salford, as 'Threlfalls Liverpool & Salford Ales'. Operations also continued at Trueman Street and, in 1888, a merger with Mathesons of Bond Street (off Vauxhall Road) took place (this brewery traded from approximately 1828, also having premises in Juvenal Street). In 1925, Threlfalls took over Thoroughgoods of Waterloo, which was formed through an amalgamation of several family concerns all named Thoroughgoods, established about 1887 at premises originally constructed by Daniel Edward Okell (Isle of Man

Strictly speaking the director was correct in his assessment: although singing and dancing and drinking after hours 'unofficially' has always gone on within various pubs, pub games were few in Liverpool. Although most customers preferred just to drink, a police report from the 1890s states various games were allowed in some public houses and are listed under the appropriate pubs; they were cards, dominoes, quoits and 'tip it'. Darts was not included and strangely only one public house was listed as allowing draughts to be played (a Threlfalls public house, 185 Netherfield Road North).

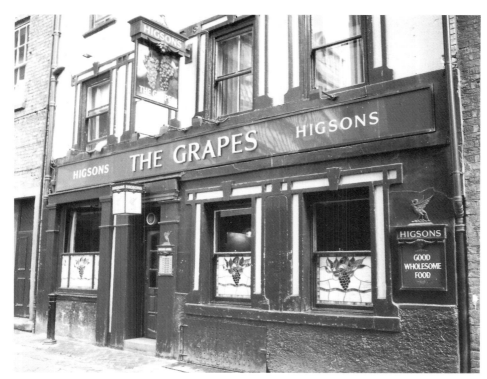

THE GRAPES, Mathew Street
This photograph is from 1994 when the pub was managed by Alan Clark. It has also been listed under the following names: in the 1850s Commercial House, 1870s Commercial Hotel, 1880s the Letters, for two years only in the 1890s Ye Old Welsh Ale Stores, then from 1898 to date the Grapes.

WALKERS/CAINS BREWERY
This view from the 1920s of Walkers in Dallam Lane, Warrington, shows a way of life that has now long vanished, as 'horsepower' was replacing horses. Walkers had a new brewery built in Dallam Lane in 1967.

In the nineteenth century, few pubs advertised their names on the outside of the establishment. When it became common practice, Threlfalls, for some reason continued to display the brewery name only. Another feature of Threlfalls was having a picture of the Queen in all their pubs.

Brewers). In the 1890s, Thoroughgoods had some 60 pubs, mainly in the Waterloo, Crosby, Southport and South Lancashire areas. In 1961, Threlfalls merged with Chester of Manchester, succumbing, in 1967, to a national takeover by Whitbread.

WALKERS/CAINS

Although Walkers Ale is brewed in Warrington, they have operated from offices in Liverpool since 1868 and, having more pubs than any other brewer in the city, can be considered as much a part of Liverpool's brewing history as any other.

A.B. Walker began the business in the 1840s, later joined by his father who was already a brewer in Ayr, Scotland. They set up in Warrington, purchasing the already established King Street Brewery and moving to Dallam Lane in 1866. They were henceforth known as Peter Walker and Son. The office acquired in Duke Street,

Liverpool, was on the site of Liverpool's first library and the company still remains there.

There was also a branch of the company at Burton (Warrington & Burton) and a brewery was in operation in Wrexham during the 1870s. During the 1840s, Robert Cain started to produce beer in Limekiln Lane, Liverpool. In about 1854 with an increase in trade, he needed larger premises, which he acquired in Wilton Street, off St Anne Street. Later he leased the premises to a Messrs. David and Matthew Warriner, Brewers, who subsequently bought them and, with the proceeds, purchased the Mersey Bry Brewery in Stanhope Street from a Rev. Hindley of St George Church, Everton who, along with his brother Robert, had inherited the premises from their father. Robert Hindley ran the business for two years after his father's death but without success. Surrounded by court property, the bry was rapidly enlarged by Robert Cain. A block named Cotters Terrace and a number of courts were cleared for expansion and the premises were upgraded with new, modern machinery and utensils, making it one of the country's foremost breweries. The company also had premises at St James Place during the 1890s and Grafton Street from 1908 to 1922.

In 1921, Robert Cain and Sons merged with Peter Walker (Warrington) and formed Walker Cain Ltd. They had only traded as the Mersey Bry for two years when, in 1923, the brewery was sold to Higsons. In 1960, the company merged with Joshua Tetley and Son Ltd of Leeds, to form Tetley Walker Ltd and, the following year, were joined by Ind Coope. Today, the company is presently part of the giant Allied Breweries Group.

Sponsorship now plays an ever increasing role in major sporting events. This team and location are unknown, but I wonder if this was an original form of sponsorship, or simply Walkers own team advertising their brew?

Since Higsons' departure, a brewery has once again opened up on the Stanhope Street site using the old name of Cains and has since been voted as having Britain's number one bitter in the Great British Beer Festival of 1991; quite an achievement for a comparatively new brewery.

Other brewers taken over by Walker Cain were:

Jopplin Breweries Ltd. Established in 1847 in Norman Street off London Road, this was located behind the White Lion public house until 1907 when taken over by Cains.

Richard Barker & Co. Listed in South John Street in the 1870s, then Fraser Street, before moving to Derby Road, Huyton, in 1889 until, with their 30 public houses, they were taken over in 1926.

James Tarbuck. Listed as 1-5 Rose Hill 1889-1914 and at 84 Richmond Row 1892-1914 when acquired by Walkers.

Harding And Parrington. Founded in Juvenal Street 1870-76, then moving to a large brewery (St James Brewery) 57-59 St James Street, at the junction of Nelson Street. (This site is now a recently built Chinese supermarket.) Bought out by Walkers in 1921 with approximately 15 public houses.

Robert Blezard. Originally started in Prescot Row, off Tithebarn Street, in 1839 and, by 1857, had acquired the Liver Brewery at the north end of Scotland Road, next to the Brewery Public House, where they remained until 1921 when taken over with 48 pubs.

There was a Thomas Blezard who also brewed at the Liver Brewery in the 1870s and was a licensee of the Liver Inn PH, Kirkdale Road. Earlier in the 19th century, there was also a George Blezard who had several public houses at various locations. All may have been related. The name 'Blezards' reappeared once again in 1987 when, ironically, Tetley sold some 80 pubs to this company. The name has once again been changed and is now known as 'Belhaven'.

James Mellor. This brewery was founded in 1823 in Hunter Street off Byrom Street; several members of the family were involved with brewing. They were taken over in 1946, although the public houses continued to display the name Mellors. They were later established as WSM.

Breweries were not only confined to brewing intoxicating liquor, a favourite drink of bygone days was ginger beer.

In the 1880s, 218-20 Netherfield Road North was listed as belonging to E. Dugdale, Ginger Beer Manufacturer. The approach was through a subterranean tunnel into a brick building standing on the steep Everton hillside. Before entering the tunnel, there was a gateway into a large courtyard where the stables and coach-house were located. The tunnel, arched over with brick, was constructed out of the rock and was some 53 feet long, 8 feet wide and just on 6 feet high. From here was the lower basement, where the barrels were stored; this area was 26 feet long, 11 feet wide and nearly 10 feet high. A tram car conveyed the barrels from here to the bottom of the tunnel.

From the lower basement were four more 'storeys'. The first level was some 26 feet in height, reached by ladder. This was used as the cooling room; when the gates at the end of the tunnel were opened, the volume of air forced up acted as a coolant. The next level was used for the storage

LION TAVERN
A highly decorated pub named after the old 'Lion' locomotive. Listed as 28 Tithebarn Street and 67 Moorfields. This view is from 1923 when the licensee was Henry Thomson. The large building on the right of the photograph displays the name Butterworth, a firm of oil merchants, while the lower portion is the Railway PH. Seen in Moorfields is the Popular Sweet Stores listed as 65, and 63 was Alan Brown, Tailor.

THE SANDON
Listed as 182 Oakfield Road close to Liverpool Football Club's ground at the junction of Houlding Street. In the early days when Everton played at the nearby Anfield ground, the pub was used by the players as a 'changing room'.

of hops and malt and also housed the boiler for generating heat to the vats, kiln and engine.

Steps to the third level led to the bottling room which was nearly 30 feet long and also contained a drying kiln. The upper level contained a steam winch, engine, main driving shafts, pulleys, malt mill, water pump and feed water heater. The general construction of the brewery was such that it could easily be converted for brewing intoxicating liquor.

Had this structure survived it would have been a fascinating piece of industrial architecture. The site of this long demolished brewery was between Nicholson Street and Hapton Street. Nicholson Street has been absorbed into landscaped gardens while Hapton Street still stands.

A typical rags to riches story is that of local brewer, John Houlding, who was a well-known and respected character. He was born in 1833 in Tenterden Street, off Scotland Road, the son of a cow-keeper. At the age of ten he attended a college in Shaw Street and it was here he gained a knowledge of arithmetic that helped achieve his later success.

He began his working life as a porter in the Exchange, then found employment in a brewery in Soho Street, where he worked as a dray man and labourer. Being an ambitious man, he soon acquired brewing skills and even worked on the accounts side of the business. By 1864, he had saved enough money to buy his first public house where he employed a manager to run it for him while he continued to work at the brewery. A few years later, he acquired another pub and, shortly after 1870, he decided to venture out on his own and purchased land in Tynemouth Street, Everton, to start his own brewery. During this period, he was offered the post of chairman of the Everton branch of the Conservative Party. This was to be the start of his

public life that would eventually earn him the title 'King John of Everton'.

Whilst his brewery thrived, he lived in a modest terrace house in nearby Rishton Street. He was soon nominated as Guardian of Everton Township and became chairman of the Mill Road Workhouse and was also on the Walton Workhouse Committee. He joined the Freemasons in 1869 and, by 1877, had become the Worshipful Master. In the same year, he was elected chairman of the West Derby Board and was heavily involved in education and 'rights' for the poor. Throughout all this he continued his business as a brewer.

In 1884, Mr Houlding was elected as a member of the City Council for the Everton and Kirkdale wards. His final accolade was that of Lord Mayor in 1897.

His far greater claim to fame was his split with Everton Football Club. Heavily involved, his pub the Sandon, close to the ground, was used as the headquarters for the club. He even moved from his home in Rishton Street and bought a house facing the ground - Stanley House on Anfield Road. After many squabbles, mainly over rent, a bitter dispute led Everton F.C. to leave their ground at Anfield and move over to Goodison Park. The football loving public thought at first this split would harm the game of football, however, a new club was formed - Liverpool Football Club. As history has proved, the fierce yet friendly rivalry between the two teams has continued to the present day. Prior to the formation of Liverpool Football Club, Everton's main local rivals were Bootle F.C., who acquired league status but sadly for one season only, 1892-93. Football is part and parcel of Liverpool life and for generations has been one of the main topics of conversation throughout local pubs.

John Houlding's brewery was finally taken over by Ind-Coope & Alsop in 1938.

Dale Street

DALE STREET (1908)

Dale Street and its vicinity, like the town in general, has seen many changes over the years. Dale Street was one of the town's original seven streets and, for centuries, the main thoroughfare in and out of the town. Ancient inns and taverns would have existed along its frontage.

With no means of transport other than horseback prior to the 1760s, inns and taverns were few and far between. One of the most notable inns of the town for travellers and visitors was the Golden Lion in Dale Street. The Golden Lion was probably of ancient date for, as long ago as the 1790s, it was described in the Liverpool Guide by W. Moss as 'formerly the largest and best inn of the town'.

Coffee houses, although plentiful from the 1790s, were

at this time a rare sight. In 1760 only one existed in the town, described as 'a small dark room in a court in Water Street up a narrow dingy passage was the common subscription coffee room, the only one then in town.'

In 1760, the first stage coach from London came directly to Liverpool once a week, the journey taking up to four days. (The first reference being, in July 1760, to any part of England from the Golden Talbot Inn near the Exchange, Liverpool.) In the same year, coaches were advertised from the Golden Fleece in Dale Street. Soon after 1760, inns and taverns became more abundant throughout the town, notably the Mill Stone And Castle, Wool Pack, White Bull and White Bull And Punchbowl in Dale Street. The Black Horse And Rainbow stood at the junction of High Street and was of extreme age, for it was demolished in the 1780s

23

The GOLDEN LION INN,& the Old Public House adjoining. Dale Stree
1828.

THE GOLDEN LION INN and THE OLD PUBLIC HOUSE, 1828.

THE ANGEL INN, Dale Street. 1830.

THE ANGEL INN, 1830.

when the area was widened and Dale Street set back from its former narrow, irregular line. Close by stood another very old pub, the Cross Keys, and others included: the Mill Stone, Castle Street; White Lion, Water Street; Wheatsheaf and White Hart, High Street, and the Crooked Billet, Tithebarn Street.

The Angel Inn, situated between North John Street and Castle Street, later became two separate establishments, the Angel Hotel and Angel Vaults. A restaurant adjoining the Angel was known as Daley's Dandelion (the name was to reappear in the 1980s when a club opened close to the original site). The first Angel closed in the 1840s, although the name was used on another structure and a section of the old building remained until the 1950s, when replaced by the present State Building.

Close by was the Manchester Arms which, together with two other buildings, were replaced by the present Temple, built in 1864-65, whilst the Colonial Building was replaced by the present Prudential Assurance Building (erected 1885-86).

Yates' Wine Lodge has long been familiar with the drinking fraternity of Liverpool. Seven existed in the city centre, presently two remain. The first was located in Colonial Chambers in the 1880s, listed simply as 'wine lodge' (although owned by Peter Yates of Oldham). This building was replaced by the present Prudential Assurance Building when the Wine Lodge ceased trading. (Back Colonial Buildings still remains, adjoining Colonial Chambers from a PH named the Oporto Vaults, possibly part of the building that Yates acquired.) Ironically, another of Yates' wine lodges, also short lived, stood close by. This was in the State Building from the 1960s until closure in the late 1970s.

The Saracens Head, closed in 1867, was situated on the south side of Dale Street, where now stands the Municipal Buildings. For many years under the ownership of Bartholomew Bretherton, it was the most important coaching inn of the town. During the early 19th century, Bretherton built up a coaching service to all parts of the country and his stables at Rainhill, Old Roan and Parr accommodated some 700 horses. He also ran coaches from the Angel and Talbot, Water Street.

The coming of the railway was the death knell for the old coaches and Mr Bretherton, who had a lucrative business of some 700 horses around 1830, was reduced to just two coaches running from the Saracens Head to Southport by 1847.

Although Dale Street was the main departure/arrival point for coaches, during the 18th and early 19th centuries many commodious inns and taverns were common in other areas. W. Moss in his *Liverpool Guide* of 1795 states:

'The largest inn is the hotel at the bottom of Lord Street.* Others were Kings Arms, Talbot Inn and London Tavern, all Water Street. Crown Inn, Redcross Street, Star and Garter, Paradise Street, Globe Tavern, John Street, others un-named were in Dale Street, High Street and Tithebarn Street.' *(probably Bates).

Although the locations of the previously mentioned inns are known, the increase in the number of the more humble public houses built from the late 18th century makes it difficult to know exactly where they all stood. The prime reason being variable street numbering (which began in 1773). For example, a street may have started 1, 2, 3, 4, etc. with 5, 6, 7, 8 facing, whilst others may have been 1, 2, 3, 4, with 8, 7, 6, 5 etc. facing.

Another confusing aspect was, when building ceased only to be resumed at a later date, the numbers would not necessarily correspond with the rest of the street. The system presently used was adopted about 1838. An example of the old numbering can be shown by the old Saracens Head, Dale Street. Although its location is known,

in a directory of 1847 it is listed as number 96, whilst others list the premises as 90, 93, and 135.

Some of the town's pubs are also now impossible to record since, in several of the early directories, pubs that did not make a contribution to the cost of the edition were omitted altogether. In a directory from 1766, seven named inns are recorded on Dale Street. They were: Golden Fleece, Woolpack, Mill Stone And Castle, Cross Keys, White Bull, Angel and the Golden Lion (note the Bull And Punchbowl and Black Horse And Rainbow are omitted). Eight years later, in 1774, twelve were listed with numbers but only six were named. Omitted were Mill Stone And Castle, Cross Keys and White Bull (although still in existence) whilst two more are named the Red Lion and the Angel And Crown. That year, 1774, with numbering only just introduced, the Golden Lion close to the Town Hall was listed as 6, whilst the Golden Fleece also close to the Town Hall was listed as 168. I am therefore using the date of '18th century' for a number of pubs and inns that may have been in existence at any date in that period.

Intermixed with the breweries mentioned earlier and the previously mentioned inns and taverns of Dale Street were the following: on the north side, 9 was the site of the previously mentioned Cross Keys. The George Hotel was built here in about 1790 and was then listed at 15. Extending to Hackins Hey, it was demolished during the 1850s, when replaced by the present Union Marine Building. A former licensed establishment in this building was the Bodega Company Limited WSM, later becoming Bodega PH then listed at 11, and now a hairdressers.

In 1870, at the other junction of Hackins Hey and Dale Street stood a spirit vault named the Palatine. Extensive alterations took place in the 1890s, when the old pub was replaced by Palatine Chambers. Further proof of the reconstruction is that 17 was listed for the first time as George Miller & Co., Printers, Palatine Chambers. A police report from the 1890s states that:

'The licensed premises consist of the ground floor and basement of Palatine Chambers. There is a door opening off the passage leading to the offices from the Dale Street entrance to the building.'

The ground floor remained as a public house named the Palatine but currently trades as the Saddle. A strong nautical decor is evident in this pub, pictures of ships from the White Star Line are displayed on the walls. Correspondence between the founder of the White Star Line, Ismay and his cousin who was a ship's master are also exhibited. The correspondence was conducted from the original 'Saddle Inn', further along Dale Street.

Thomas Rigby (1815-86) came to Liverpool, in 1830, from Lowton Common near Newton-le-Willows. At the age of 30, he commenced business at the corner of Crosshall Street and Whitechapel as a Wholesale and Retail Wine and Spirit dealer, eventually owning a large number of pubs around the town. As his prosperity grew, he went into politics and, in 1858, he contested but lost St Paul's Ward to Mr J. Clerk. Thomas Rigby challenged Clerk's qualifications and, after two years' litigation, he gained the seat. In 1861, he was defeated by Mr J.B. Spence and, in 1863, he tried to take Vauxhall Ward and was again defeated. Finally, in 1864, he successfully opposed Mr Robert Bradbury in St Paul's Ward. As a devoted Conservative, Thomas Rigby's role for serving his party was soon appreciated and, in 1868, he became Alderman.

VERNON ARMS
Listed as 69 Dale Street and 1 Vernon Street. Previously a WSV that stood between Vernon Street and Nixon Place (a former alley off Dale Street). When Vernon Chambers was built in the late 19th century, the old WSV and Nixon Place were both demolished. Prior to the construction of the WSV (probably 1850s) the Saddle Inn stood on this site and was listed as 9 Vernon Street and 67a Dale Street (151 in 1820s).

Vernon Arms as it is today.

Number 19 Dale Street was part of Rigby's Building and warehouses behind the pub included BH, offices and bottling stores and were also connected with Ye Hole In The Wall. Extensive alterations occurred once more during the 1920s when the building resembled that of today. Thomas Rigby owned the premises from approximately 1852 until his death in 1886, although he was never listed as victualler, and it is somewhat strange that, in the 1875 list, 6 Dale Street, almost facing, had Martha E. Rigby listed as proprietress.

In common with numerous pubs, the premises were not named in any directories, which list only the various victuallers. Probably after the reconstruction around 1923 the premises were listed as Rigby's. Apparently, the premises were frequented by Horatio Nelson during the 1790s and a section of the pub, Nelson's Room, is dedicated to him. A letter written by Nelson was displayed for many years in this room but sadly disappeared some years ago.

In the 1880s, Charles Millward described this pub as one of the most popular, well-conducted establishments in the town:

'As far as my experience goes, the barmen have always been singularly smart, active, and attentive. It was a peculiar feature in all the houses owned by Mr. Rigby that barmen were employed in preference to barmaids, and strict rules were laid down for their guidance in conducting the business. The Dale Street snuggery has had some noteworthy men as managers.'

Charles Millward also illustrated an incident in the life of a 19th-century landlord who ran the Saddle Inn, concerning a deceptive act that occurred during the heyday of the inn, which was one of the town's principal hotels of the last century. With a section in Vernon Street containing mews and stables, it was one of the prime 'stage coach inns' on Dale Street:

'Landlords were wide awake in those days, and open as now to turn opportunities to account. It will be more than 50 years ago that two gentlemen in the wool trade, who resided in Halifax, and were in the habit of making periodical visits to Liverpool, arrived one day, with their horses and goods, and put up as usual at the Saddle. They had occasion, however, to journey to Dublin and, in the absence of steamboats, had to make the uncertain voyage in a sailing vessel. Their animals were duly left to the landlord's faithful care, and the two friends embarked. Favourable winds and other propitious circumstances wafted them to Ireland and back in an unusually short time. Their speedy return was unexpected, but was cheerfully welcomed by mine host. Not so, however, was their proposed early departure on their homeward journey. The evening was fine and bright and, after a seasonable rest and an excellent dinner, the gentlemen determined to make as far as Warrington for the night. It was natural that "Boniface" should be desirous of detaining his guests if possible, but his efforts to dissuade them from leaving were unusually earnest. However, the travellers started, but their nags seemed to have held the same opinion as the landlord, and did not do their work with their usual alacrity. On reaching the Warrington stables and alighting, the animals' laziness was mentioned to the hotelier. That functionary looked up and, giving a wink of his eye and a knowing smile, said, "Not go well, indeed, I should think not. What horses would, as done what they have; why, this, is the third time they've been here today." That quick passage to Ireland and back let these travellers into a secret. It was clear that mine host of the Saddle made the best use of his patrons' animals for his own emoluments when he thought the opportunity served.'

It is difficult to imagine the squalid buildings that once

existed off Dale Street during the early years of the nineteenth century. One avenue, Queens Avenue, still remains as a quaint thoroughfare from Dale Street to Castle Street. This replaced a number of courts including Swift Court and Slater Court. Another thoroughfare close to Queens Avenue is Sweeting Street, where an old inn was located at 8, once listed as the Old House At Home then Dean Swift's Box. It was probably in existence when Sweeting Street had an earlier name of Elbow Lane. The premises may have taken this name when the nearby Dean Swift's Snuff Box was demolished. Surprisingly, although long closed as a pub, together with the adjoining buildings they are still standing.

The Red Lion stood on the junction of the block on Dale Street between Chorley Court and Fontenoy Street. The block at the other junction of Chorley Court (145-147) was a former pub named Horse And Jockey. This block and slum dwellings of Chorley Court were demolished in the 1930s to be replaced by the present Blackburn Chambers. Chorley Court was the birth place of Robert Morris, 1734-1806; born in poverty he emigrated to America when only thirteen and prospered to become one of America's greatest financiers. A signatory of the Declaration of Independence, his other achievements included Superintendent of Finance in the Congress, Head of the Navy Department and he established the Bank of North America, the oldest financial institution in America.

Ironically, despite his rags to riches story, he died as he was born - in poverty, in a debtor's prison in Philadelphia.

In the first half of the nineteenth century, three inns were located on the site where the Municipal Buildings now stand: Old White Lion Inn, Saracens Head and Flying Horse. By 1855 they, and other property, were all demolished and the land remained vacant until 1857, when the town's first permanent circus opened upon this site (before this date only travelling circuses were seen). The proprietor was Charles Hengler, a Dane by birth. It was an instant success and, according to a contemporary account, 'the cheers of the vast audience might almost have been heard in the town hall. They were distinctly heard at the Saddle Hotel, and in the slummy streets leading into still more slummy Whitechapel.' On that first day, March 16, 1857, among the acts were four of the world's greatest clowns of the time. Exactly 110 years later, a type of entertainment unknown to the Victorian masses was in full swing - 'Beatlemania'. In that year, 1967, one of the songs on the album 'Sgt. Pepper's Lonely Hearts Club Band' was 'Mr Kite', in which one of the lines is: 'The Hendersons will all be there, late of Paplo Fanques fair.' M. Henderson was known as Clown Fanques, who was one of the four clowns who appeared 110 years earlier on the opening day.

Despite its popularity, the final equestrian performance was in March 1861, as the Corporation had acquired the land for the construction of the Municipal Buildings. A new

WILLIAM BROWN STREET
At the foot of Dale Street is one of the town's most eminent streets - William Brown Street. There is not a public house to be found amongst the magnificent buildings of today although they were once abundant. This 1898 view shows the Leicester Hotel, located at the junction with Liversley Place. A sign over the door reads 'beds' whilst on the window 'Free Storage For Bicycles'. Note the large advertisement on the adjoining shop for Ogden's Guinea Gold Cigarettes (formerly BH & eating house). The building at the other junction of Liversley Place was the Bill Posting Company and, as seen, a good advert in itself. Previously this was the Victoria Tavern with, adjoining it, the Angel Inn. In the 1850s, 21-23 was listed as a free public library and museum. The library was rebuilt and renamed the William Brown Library and Museum in 1860, about the same time Shaws Brow was renamed William Brown Street. The lower portion of the street, including Liversley Place, was replaced by the College of Technology in 1902.

HENGLER'S CIRCUS
Hengler's Circus on the site of the Municipal Buildings, Dale Street, 1859.

retains its original use. The blocks adjoining Westminster Chambers, however, are now long demolished. The British Workman Public House Co. Ltd, a round shaped building, was located at the junction with Preston Street. Prior to the construction of this building in the 1880s, it was a pub named the Stanley Arms. Further along was the former Coates Hotel, which was on the site of a long forgotten pub, the Golden Lion Hotel. An 1892 police report concerning the Golden Lion noted: 'There is a door at the Manchester Street end of the entry which is apparently not kept locked.'

In Dale Street today, the only old pubs remaining are the Saddle, Rigbys, Vernon Arms, Excelsior and the Ship And Mitre - all on the north side. The south side was extensively rebuilt in the late 19th and early 20th centuries and no old pubs remain on that side, although two modern structures, the Angel and Dandy's Dandelion, reflect the past in name only.

DALE STREET VICINITY

Eberle Street (formally William Street) is one of the narrow streets off Dale Street, renamed after a well-known 19th-century Liverpool victualler, Philip Eberle, who was born in Germany, although a British subject. Eberle was originally a barman who worked his way up in such hotels as the Waterloo and the Victoria, acquiring skills as a chef on the way. His first tenancy was a pub in South John Street named the Shippers. He eventually became licensee of the Royal and Royal Alexander, both in Dale Street, also acquiring the Bath Hotel, South Road, Waterloo.

site was found quickly in Newington, which opened in October 1861. However, in its new location it never quite captured the previous fervour and Charles Hengler left Liverpool and went on to success in London, Glasgow, Dublin and elsewhere. Having a fondness for Liverpool and in fulfilling a long-standing promise to 'erect a cirque worthy of this large and appreciative community', Charles Hengler returned to Liverpool where he had built the handsome and commodious Hippodrome on West Derby Road. It opened in 1876 and flourished as one of the town's main attractions until its final demise in 1901. The following year after reconstruction, the building opened as the Royal Hippodrome Theatre Of Varieties. This remained until 1931, when it was converted to a picture house named the Royal Hippodrome. Thriving for nearly 40 years, it closed its doors in 1970. The building then remained empty and derelict for 14 years until it was finally demolished in 1984. A modern public house named the Hippodrome in nearby Everton Road along with modern housing in Hengler's Close are the only reminders of past nights of thrills and laughter.

The Gas Light Tavern stood on a portion of Dale Street between Crosshall Street and Preston Street named Westminster Chambers, built in 1880. It was earlier named the Enterprise American Hardware Company and still trades as a hardware shop, whilst the solicitors' office above the shop

JUSTICE
Listed as 113-115 Dale Street and 2 Hatton Garden. Named after the nearby magistrates courts when built in the 1860s on the site of a tobacco factory. It was demolished in the 1960s.

FENWICK TAVERN
This is located in Fenwick Street which is parallel to Castle Street. Generally thought to be one of the town's oldest pubs, in fact it only dates back to around 1850, although a pub on the same site was built in the reign of George III (1760-1820) named the St George Inn and Eagle Tavern, which was long called Lathoms after a former manager.

A glimpse of the way of life for the more well-to-do victuallers of the mid-19th century can be illustrated by the census from 1861 concerning the Bath Hotel: 'Philip Eberle, aged 37, hotel keeper, with son, four visitors and eight servants (barmaid, two waitresses, cook, bar keeper and family).'

During the 1860s, the Bath Hotel changed name to the Marine Hotel, which still trades. In the street named after him, he acquired the City Hall which, in the 1890s, was registered as the Eberle Hotel And Restaurant Co. and at that time licensed for music, singing and other entertainments. The premises were later named the Carlton Hall And Restaurant. Despite alterations over the years, the premises continued to be used as a music venue, still named the Carlton Hall and in the 1960s was listed as the Carlton Masonic Hall. It has since been a night club and a health club. Once again I must mention the destruction of our city. Leather Lane and its immediate vicinity is one of the all too rare districts of Liverpool still reminiscent of the past, with quaint narrow alleys once so abundant in the city centre.

The Liverpool Tram was located at 14 Tempest Hey at the junction of Ryley's Gardens, demolished in the 1980s and now the site of a car park. The interior was shaped like an old tram car and pictures of old Liverpool trams adorned the walls. Many former town drinkers would not be aware of this pub, as it was only in existence from 1973 to 1980. The licensee was Mary Lee, who held it for its duration. The premises were previously listed as a florists. Next door stood the Brunswick Oyster Bar, which has traded for many years.

Ye Hole In The Wall was listed as 4-6 Hackins Hey and is reputedly the oldest pub in the city centre, although this is difficult to ascertain. A date of 1726 is on its facade although this may not be genuine. The present Rigby's Building is probably no older than 1850: the date would, therefore, be that of an earlier building on the same site. The public house is more confusing as it is supposed to be built on the site of an old Quaker Meeting House. A Quaker Meeting House is recorded in 1709 and, in the 1708 rate assessment, is recorded as having a burial ground underneath. It was used by the Quakers until 1791, when they moved to Hunter Street. The premises then had various uses and, in 1813, they were in use as a school until 1861. The premises were then sold and demolished. Therefore, the public house would have to have been built after 1861. A probable explanation for the date is that it may have been in existence from 1726, either alongside or close to the old Quaker Meeting House.

The meeting house was in fact higher up Hackins Hey at the junction of Quakers Alley. A map from 1850 has the Stanley PH listed as 6 (37 in 1829) on this site, whilst 15 the Conway Castle and 10 Denbigh Castle are both named. A police report from 1892 does not even name the premises yet names both the Conway Castle and Denbigh Castle and a map of 1875 names the same two pubs but lists 2-6 as WSM. Its present name does not appear in any directories until shortly before the First World War. Prior to the 1850s, a pile of warehouses surrounded it and it is possible this pub was a lower section of a former warehouse. There are two facts that may verify this theory: firstly, the 'cellar' is located above the pub and, secondly, during the 1840s, Elizabeth Fleetwood, Victualler, was listed as having two warehouses in Hackins Hey on or close to the present site. Earlier a BH had been listed (possibly part of a warehouse). In 1799, the premises were owned by a Samuel Chesshyre and a document of the time stated that the ground floor was unbuilt. The licensed premises from records appear to have been first listed c.1740, and it is interesting to note that in the town's first directory of 1766, Carl Fleetwood, Brewer, was listed in Dale Street (probably the Saddle), whilst Mary Fleetwood was listed as Tavern Keeper, Exchange Coffee House, Water Street. A number of breweries also existed in Hackins Hey with 13-15 listed to Thomas Scott in the 1790s (probably a different

OLD SCOTCH HOUSE/EXCELSIOR
This building was listed as a PH in the last century, then in the 1890s named the Corporation Hotel. Later it acquired another name, the Old Scotch House, listed as 123 Dale Street at the corner of Johnson Street. At the other junction of Johnson Street stood the Excelsior, listed as 119 Dale Street. This pub was demolished in the 1960s and subsequently the Old Scotch House took the name Excelsior, open to date. The photograph is from 1908 (Corporation Hotel) when the manageress was Alice Maud Cleaver and features an old open-top bus waiting to take a part for a day trip to Buxton. Also shown is the rear of another bus outside the adjoining premises to the pub, a warehouse belonging to Collingwood Motors, the company organising the trips. On the wall is an advert for trips to Blackpool. The premises are now long demolished, replaced by offices.

location to the present 15, Conway Castle). The date 1726 displayed on the pub (the same as Rigby's) could be the date O'Donnell's Whisky Merchants were founded who were eventually taken over by Rigby's. Incidentally, this was the last pub in the city to lose the old custom of 'men only', with the passing of the Sex Discrimination Act of 1975.

There is no doubt that Ye Hole In The Wall is exceedingly old, which raises a difficult question - which is the oldest pub? The Fenwick, although old, had replaced an earlier pub, as is the case with Rigby's. Ye Cracke in Rice Street, although an old building, was only licensed around 1850. The Pig & Whistle, Covent Garden, and the Munro in Duke Street are both from the 18th century, although the former was originally a private house. A date of 1675 is displayed on the Central, Ranelagh Street, although this again is possibly from when it was a private residence. The King Edward, King Edward Street, built around the time of the First World War, has had at least two other buildings preceding it. Many other city centre pubs could be included, although of 'present' buildings Ye Hole In The Wall probably lays claim to being the oldest.

Away from the city centre, the Honky Tonk, Scotland Road, claims to have been established in 1740. Pubs in the suburbs are in a similar position to those in the city centre, many having replaced earlier inns. The Childwall Abbey, for example, appears from records to be the renovated Chapel of St Thomas the Martyr, built in 1484. The Woolton Coffee House is probably the oldest 'dated' pub, having on its wall a date stone of 1641.

Returning to the cluster of streets around Moorfields, only a few old buildings remain near Tithebarn Street including the Lion Tavern listed as 98 Tithebarn Street and 68 Moorfields. The pub has also been listed in the 1930s

POSTE HOUSE
Listed as 23 Cumberland Street, a narrow street between Dale Street and Victoria Street. Originally a private house belonging to one of the town's former merchants, it became a popular tavern in the early 19th century. It was patronised in those days by a mixed clientele, from sea captains to seafarers and town councillors to artisans. One day, in 1846, two famous customers were Prince Louis Napoleon (later Emperor of France) and Sir John Gerrard, the Earl of Sefton.

MATHEW STREET/RAINFORD GARDENS

Temple Court leads into a small section of the city centre that has managed to retain much of its original character. Mathew Street is now on the tourist trail for visitors to the city due to the fact it once housed the Cavern Club, made famous by the Beatles. (Needless to say the premises were demolished in the 1970s.) Rainford Gardens is where a well-known city centre pub, White Star, can still be found, while the pub in Button Street, formerly the Old House At Home, and the adjoining Zinc Worker Premises were demolished in the early 1860s and replaced by a warehouse that still stands. The Old House At Home was earlier named the Golden Fleece. The Vine Hotel was located at the other end of Button Street at the junction with Rainford Square, and was also demolished in the early 1860s to be replaced by warehouses (remaining to date). The actual corner has most recently been in use as Macca's Bar, which is closed at the time of writing.

WHITE STAR, Rainford Gardens.

and 1960s as the Moorfields Inn. Pre-war it was listed as a restaurant, earlier as a BH.

Cheapside contained various breweries including one of the first in Liverpool owned by the Harvey family, the last

closing in 1912. Currently only the Rose & Crown and United Powers trade as pubs, while the building that was the Majestic now houses a firm of solicitors. All the others were cleared many years ago, none were in existence by the 1880s and two, the Friendship Tavern and Black Horse, existed on the present site of the city's main Bridewell, built in the 1860s.

The North Street area is also unrecognisable from its 19th-century sordidness. A police report of the 1890s about a BH in the nearby Johnson Street, later named the Snuff Box commented that:

'This house has not been altogether satisfactorily conducted during the past year. The licensee left the premises in June last, and the police finding the business still carried on made enquiries and ascertained that the person in possession had no authority to sell. Proceedings were taken against the person in charge:- convictions on three informations followed.'

The district south of Dale Street was a huge slum area as far as Whitechapel which was cleared from the 1860s. One of the results of this was a new street laid out to improve the flow of traffic. Named Victoria Street, it soon became built up with new office and commercial premises. In front of the present Fruit Exchange the street forms a gentle curve, this is a legacy from pre-Victoria Street days when it was named Temple Court.

The round shaped building at the corner with Temple Court remains the oldest building on Victoria Street, approximately 200 years old and presently in use as a restaurant. It was originally built as a private house and probably connected with the nearby St Catharine's Chapel which opened in 1775 (the first structure of any significance in this vicinity, it was demolished c.1820). An earlier structure, the Octagon Temple had opened on this site in 1763, giving its name to the surrounding thoroughfares: Temple Lane, Temple Street, Temple Court and Temple Buildings. The building (which houses the present restaurant) was formerly known as Fishers Building, probably originating from the last century when the premises were occupied by a firm of solicitors named Fisher And Stone.

The Canton was a well-patronised pub in Victorian Liverpool and was frequented by many of the town's councillors of the day. One of its former well-known patrons was a Mr John Hignett who ran a snuff mill in the adjoining Temple Court; his Hignett's Mixture was not only popular locally, but nationwide and made him a very wealthy man.

The Canton, together with the rest of Temple Court, was cleared to make way for the present Fruit And Produce Building. Temple Court was covered over by Victoria Street and relocated to its present position. From the late 1880s,

VICTORIA STREET, looking towards North John Street
On the left-hand side, on the corner of Temple Court, the building with the rounded facade is the oldest on Victoria Street. The adjoining building is the Fruit and Produce Building. This was the site of the Canton public house.

VICTORIA STREET, looking towards Dale Street

When the old property was cleared to make way for Victoria Street, one of the alleys that disappeared was Pothouse Lane, the approximate site of which is now the junction of Stanley Street and Victoria Street, where the Lisbon now stands. The Lisbon Grill was well known for its adventurous cuisine, featuring both frogs' legs and escargot.

the pub's name, however, lived on facing its original site at 14 Temple Lane, where the premises had entrances in Temple Lane and Temple Buildings. Prior to this date, 14 was listed as the Temple Restaurant and, early in the last century, a public house named the Cheshire Cheese with access in Temple Lane and Progress Place (later Temple Buildings). The pub itself was then named the New Canton and remains open as a nightclub, the Curzon.

Commercial Building, built in the 1880s, had connections with the fruit trade and stands at the junction of Victoria Street facing the restaurant previously mentioned at the other corner of Temple Court. The cellars are very small with extremely thick walls and were unlike cellars used in a PH. In fact, they were used to store gunpowder during the last century, hence the small, solid construction. Behind the building is a former Crown Post Office, presently just a shell, its upper floors sadly destroyed during the Second World War.

WHITECHAPEL

Several pubs lined Sir Thomas Buildings, as well as three breweries and four BHs, along with a tobacco factory, a number of soaperies and warehouses and even a Welsh chapel, standing amongst court property. All the above property, with the exception of the Welsh chapel, was cleared during the 1850s and '60s as part of the complete transformation of the Dale Street vicinity. The old Sir Thomas Buildings was then widened and was given its present name of Sir Thomas Street. Since the reconstruction of the street, only one public house remains on Sir Thomas Street: the New Court, earlier the Court Restaurant. A police report from 1892, when it was still listed as 3 Sir Thomas Buildings, states: 'A room 24 feet x 21 feet on the ground floor has been added as a luncheon bar. Plans submitted and approved by the justices.'

The building at the junction of Whitechapel and Crosshall Street was demolished in 1995. The whole block is a triangular shape bounded by Whitechapel, Crosshall Street and Victoria Street and is now being redeveloped as office space. With the exception of the corner building, all this property formerly belonged to the Liverpool Daily Post and Echo before they moved to new premises in Old Hall Street. The corner block was in fact a large, flamboyant public house named the Swan, which ceased trading as long ago as 1912. A 'gate' separates the rest of the block which hides a cobbled area, once a section of Preston Street when it led into Whitechapel (it now terminates at Victoria Street from Dale Street). The former pub, 79 Whitechapel, is therefore located between Crosshall Street and Preston Street.

Two pubs once stood on this site, the Swan and Walsh's WSV (formerly the Old House At Home) at the junction of

Preston Street. The Swan was the first tenancy of Thomas Rigby. When the old property was demolished, Mr Rigby had a large, grandiose public house built, still named the Swan, to replace the two pubs and shops; it was demolished in 1995.

On the east-side of Whitechapel, before the massive reconstruction of the area in the mid-19th century, Crosshall Street was much narrower and contained eleven public houses. One of its former pubs is featured in the Guinness Book of Records. This was the Beehive, situated close to the junction with Shaw Hill Street. The reason? Considering the slum district that it once was, it is not surprising that a record was set by a bull terrier dog named 'Jenny Lind', which killed some 500 rats in 90 minutes in a rat pit behind the pub.

Next to the pub was the Stag And Partridge SV, and some seven narrow, dingy courts stood off the street down to Whitechapel when this record was made in 1853. The Lady Of The Lake was previously named the Wheatsheaf, formerly listed as 35 Preston Street at the junction of Shaw

SHAKESPEARE HOTEL
Listed as 43 Whitechapel. During the last century this hotel was one of the many magnificent Victorian buildings that were constructed during the heyday of Liverpool's prosperity. Here the hotel is in its last stage of demolition as a result of war damage.

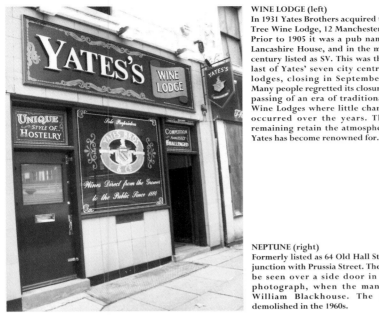

WINE LODGE (left)
In 1931 Yates Brothers acquired the Oak Tree Wine Lodge, 12 Manchester Street. Prior to 1905 it was a pub named the Lancashire House, and in the mid-19th century listed as SV. This was the third last of Yates' seven city centre Wine lodges, closing in September 1993. Many people regretted its closure as the passing of an era of traditional-style Wine Lodges where little change had occurred over the years. The two remaining retain the atmosphere that Yates has become renowned for.

NEPTUNE (right)
Formerly listed as 64 Old Hall Street at the junction with Prussia Street. The name can be seen over a side door in this 1912 photograph, when the manager was William Blackhouse. The pub was demolished in the 1960s.

Hill Street. Mass demolition of the vicinity swept away Shaw Hill Street, which led from Peter Street into a street named Spitalfields behind Manchester Street. Some warehouses still remain, with the site of the pub now a car park.

During the nineteenth century, Peter Street, which is now just a narrow alley alongside the former Midland Goods Depot from Whitechapel to Victoria Street, ran approximately a further 100 yards into what is now a car park behind the Municipal Buildings and was once the rear of the Saracens Head where extensive stables stood.

A number of pubs featured in this book are now but a memory and so too is the huge number of characters that once frequented them. To mention them all would warrant a book in itself and, sadly, like the pubs themselves, characters are becoming rarer. The Wine Lodges arguably had more characters than any other establishment and, among the numerous people classed in that category, I will mention just one that I knew personally. Bridget Donovan with her daughter Eileen frequented the Manchester Street premises day and night for many years and always sat in the same seats. Nellie Holmes, who managed the pub for some twenty years, recalls that Bridget Donovan drank there when she first started work in the wine lodge. With age taking its toll, by the early 1990s she was confined to a wheelchair but still managed to turn up with her daughter wheeling her in until, sadly, she passed away shortly before her 98th birthday and, ironically, just weeks before her beloved local closed.

A large public house, the Canton, not to be confused with the one in Victoria Street, was prominent at the junction of Whitechapel. The Kings Arms and the former Music Hall PH were situated at the junction with St Johns Lane. On the north side of Manchester Street was a public

house, the Stanley Arms, renamed the Cumberland Hotel when acquired by Yates Brothers in about 1912 and located almost facing their other premises (Oak Tree Wine Lodge). Statues of Queen Mary and King George V stood on the original site of the Cumberland Hotel on Manchester Street (they were relocated from the tunnel entrance during the 1960s when a new flyover was built). To celebrate the 60th anniversary of the opening of the Mersey Tunnel, the statues have once again returned to their original site at the tunnel entrance.

Travelling north of Dale Street, Old Hall Street was one of the town's original streets, for centuries a private road leading to the 'Old Hall'. With the growth of industry in the area in the last century, it deteriorated into a most squalid quarter of the town and, in common with the rest of the city centre, housed numerous public houses. More recently, the street has become part of the business quarter and few pubs remain, two of those that have disappeared are the Neptune and the Beehive.

Union Street was a narrow street located off Old Hall Street. It still stands today but is very different from the 1860s, when there were six pubs all within close proximity. Two listed boarding houses were former pubs, Filde Tavern and Holyhead Harbour (by the 1890s this was listed as the Welsh Harp). The London Hotel & Restaurant was later the Grapes PH. 3 Union Street was the Union Vaults at the junction with Old Hall Street; this, along with the Virginia Vaults at the Fazakerley Street junction was replaced by a bank. After the bank's closure, part of the building is now in use as licensed premises named Brokers.

One old structure managed to survive when Union Street was redeveloped during the 1960s and '70s. It is the type of building one would walk past without even noticing it, as it is sandwiched between Irwell Chambers East and

BEEHIVE
Listed as 74 Old Hall Street and situated a little more northward than the Neptune, this old photograph displays Thomas Shaw Wine and Spirits stores. He was manager of the premises between 1889 and 1913. Earlier named Dominica Hotel, this old pub was also demolished in the 1960s. The two shops shown on this view were: 72 William Jones & Co., Chemists, and 76 James Hughes, Linen Draper.

Irwell Chambers West on the south side of the street. This building is the London Hotel (later Grapes). All the other property beyond this on the south side of the street was demolished in the 1870s for the construction of Irwell Chambers West and Spellow Place was relocated to its present site. The premises were vacant in 1994.

The Old Stile House was listed as 9 Chapel Street and 1 Old Church Yard. A well-known pub situated close to the Parish Church of Our Lady & St Nicholas, it was replaced by a new office block in the 1980s. In the last century there was also a well-known pub, Cunninghams, named after a character and celebrated victualler of his day. Charles Millward in one of his articles recalled that it was in George Cunningham's pub he first tasted real London Stout out of pewter tankards.

The Railway, Tithebarn Street, is one of a few pubs left that was typical of the elevated structures built in the city centre in the mid-19th century, where the rooms above would have been rented dwellings. The street once contained some 30 PHs, although only a handful are left.

As historical knowledge is passed down through generations both orally and written, interpretations may vary and facts discounted or reexamined to form new theories. Although rather insignificant, the following mistake concerning the Bears Paw was written in the *Liverpool Citizen*, a 19th-century paper, normally correct in its reporting. The article included a brief history of pub signs.

From time immemorial, 'trades' people have used signs as a means of identification, originally to display their wares to an illiterate population and, as long ago as 1393, Richard II passed a law forcing every publican to hang out a business sign. Early signs were often taken from coats of arms from old, established families, e.g. Sefton, Derby etc. Others originated from royalty, e.g. King, Queen, Duke etc. Animals, with their numerous permutations, were common, e.g. Bear And Staff, Lion And Unicorn, Dog And Partridge etc. Colour was and still is frequently found, e.g. White Lion, Red Lion (the latter being the most popular pub name in this country, although locally the most common name was the Grapes). 'Bear' colours included black, white, brown, red and even green, similarly colours were used for dogs, cats, eagles, swans etc.

For all the numerous animal signs, according to the *Liverpool Citizen*, the town was unique in that an inn was named after one part of an animal's anatomy as the following report depicts:

'A unique exception exists in Liverpool and that is the case of the Bears Paw. We know of no other instance in which that portion of the brute's anatomy has been chosen as a sign to the rejection of the rest of the body.'

In fact, the name was in existence throughout the country and it can be presumed when this was written 100 years ago it would have caused some minor arguments in the pubs (there was a pub of the same name listed in Chorley Street in 1829). A pub open to date listed as 139 Paddington and 62 Irvine Street also had this name when the article was written and in fact still has, although pre-1880s it was named the Royal Duke.

The inn in question was located in Tithebarn Street and was so named about 1830, previously having been part of the European Eating House. It remained until about 1857 when, along with all the surrounding property, it was demolished. A new Bears Paw was opened by the same owners in Castle Street for a short spell then, in approximately 1881, it moved to Lord Street where it remained until destroyed during the war. New premises lower down Lord Street, at the junction of Dorans Lane, were later opened as the New Bears Paw, remaining until the 1980s when the original name was dropped in favour of Harrington's then, in 1991, McCartney's Bar. Incidentally, when the new premises were opened in Lord Street, the proprietor was John Cobham, whose father apparently founded the original and, at the entrance, used to stand a huge, stuffed bear which stood holding out a snuff box. Supposedly it had been shot by John Cobham, which was possible as, before opening the premises, he was an adventurer in America and Australia.

WEDDING HOUSE
Listed as 24 Pownall Square at the junction of Highfield Street. The view is from Pownall Square taken some time between 1896 and 1905 when the manager was Edwin Smith.

ROSE AND CROWN
Listed as 30-32 Highfield Street at the junction of Pownall Square. The photograph is from the 1920s when the pub was managed by Hugh McNeill. Though closed in 1993, when surrounded by municipal tenements awaiting demolition, the property has since reopened as licensed premises.

CHAPEL STREET
The junction of Chapel Street and New Quay. The massive public house on the corner was the Princes. Next door to the adjoining warehouse is another ornate pub, the British Queen. All this property was demolished to create a branch entry for the Mersey Tunnel.

RISING SUN
Listed as 77 Tithebarn Street at the junction of Smithfield Street. The pre-First World War photograph has the name Hunters clearly written on the window. This was Marcella Hunter, licensee from 1898 to 1918. During the last century 77 was listed as the unusually named Revolving Lamp PH (although it may have been at a different location).

The Rising Sun today.

BRUNSWICK VAULTS (earlier Brunswick Stores)
Listed as 69 and situated at the junction of Highfield Street. This view is from 1923 when the licensee was James White. The shop adjoining on Tithebarn Street was a tobacconist belonging to William Norman. This is now the site of a car park which separates the pub from the Rising Sun. The shop in Highfield Street was a chandlers belonging to Arthur Titchmarch and has also been demolished.

GREAT EASTERN, 1890s
Listed as 28 Smithfield Street and 1-3 Cockspur Street. This picture was taken in the 1890s when managed by Edwin Cole. At its height Smithfield Street contained a number of breweries and 12 public houses.

GREAT EASTERN, 1920s
The premises appear to have been rebuilt, as this view from the 1920s is completely different from the 1890s view. The pub was demolished in the 1960s.

Lime Street

LIME STREET STATION
The Royal Hotel in its final days before the block was demolished to make way for a retail and office development.

Lime Street was originally Liverpool's notorious red light district, where 'ladies of the night' would parade along its length and offer their services to the numerous seamen who were attracted to the area. In many public houses, prostitution was rife, particularly during the aptly named 'naughty '90s' (referring to the 1890s). I have not listed the police reports on prostitution individually because all the licensed premises of the street were frequented by prostitutes and all the licensees of the establishments had either been warned or prosecuted at some time or other.

Originally named Limekiln Lane, after lime kilns which stood on the site of the present railway station, building mainly commenced in Lime Street from the 1790s and it rapidly became a main thoroughfare. The section of Lime Street between Elliot Street and Roe Street was named St George's Place. Originally this site contained two hotels, Queens Hotel and Washington Hotel. The Queens had an open arcade through the premises into Rose Street to its rear, which ran alongside the old market. Throughout the last century, after various alterations and redevelopment, the Queens was taken over by the Washington. Although named St George's Place, the whole block was locally known as 'Queens Arcade'. The Washington Hotel was listed as 9 Queens Arcade. The proprietor of the hotel from 1929 through to the 1950s was Ellen Guller. An advertisement from the 1930s for the hotel gives the tariff for the rooms: 'Bed & Breakfast 1st Floor 9/6d, 2nd Floor 8/6d.'

Prior to demolition in the 1960s, this former well-known section of Lime Street also contained the Douglas Hotel, Caledonian PH, St George's Hotel and the Imperial

LIME STREET / ST GEORGE'S PLACE
From right to left: Washington Hotel, Imperial Hotel and St George's Hotel.

The same buildings photographed at night showing the famous neon lights.

A beer house in Rose Street. Located behind the Queens Hotel, the premises finally closed in the 1930s.

CALEDONIAN
Listed as 34 Lime Street. The American Bar was not the only one in Lime Street to bear this title, three separate pubs had the name at different periods. The Caledonian was originally the American Hotel as long ago as the 1840s. It was then renamed the Albany before finally being called the Caledonian in the 1860s.

SAVOY
Listed as 27-29 Lime Street. Between Gloucester Street and Skelhorne Street once stood a small, narrow street named Hanley Street, which contained court property. Two pubs stood on the corner of Hanley Street and Lime Street: the Grand Junction Hotel and the Savoy. The Savoy, photographed in 1906 when the manager was Henry George Kerrison, had an earlier name of Lime Street Vaults. Strangely, for only one year, 1909, the pub was listed as the Willow Bank Hotel. Unfortunately, like so many others, it was demolished during the early 1960s.

43

ST GEORGE'S

Listed as 18-20 Lime Street. This photograph taken before the First World War had the name of the hotel superimposed on it and shows the various premises on the ground floor including Turkish Baths, restaurant and the booking office for the Great Western Railway. Previously named the Grand Hotel, amongst former function rooms which this hotel once housed were the Shamrock Social Club in the 1950s and the Marionette Club during the 1940s. The site once again accommodates a hotel with the same name, St George's.

ROYAL HOTEL

Listed as 15-19 Lime Street. This view from the 1890s shows the Royal Hotel with the name 'Bernards' on the frontage. This was the manager's name, George Bernard, licensee from 1880 until 1894, prior to it being named the Royal Railway Hotel; it became the Royal Hotel in 1889.

ROYAL HOTEL

This photograph, taken in the 1960s, shows the pub being demolished along with the whole block. With a little foresight and instead of constructing a single deck of shops this could have become an attractive area had it been landscaped, maybe with a fountain and flowerbeds to enhance the wonderful curve of the station roof which now can hardly be seen from Lime Street.

Hotel. Lime Street was a spectacle of neon lights at night, particularly St George's Place where one of the attractions was the Guinness Clock.

The Grapes/Empire Theatre was listed as 7-9 on the east side of Lime Street. This was one of the street's earliest pubs, situated where the present Empire Theatre stands. In the early years of the last century, it stood as a plain brick house with steps leading to it, probably a private residence at that time. It was listed pre-1850s as the Worcestershire House.

Alongside the pub stood a coach makers and to its rear and side, as far as Pudsey Street, were stables and mews (owned by the proprietor of the pub for many years). Its isolation ceased in 1866, when a new theatre opened alongside - the New Prince of Wales Theatre and Italian Opera House (the name was only kept for a year when it became the Royal Alexandra Theatre and Opera House). Finally, in 1895, the theatre took its present title, the Empire. It was during this time that the old Grapes closed as a public house with the building remaining. During the 1890s, it was a hatters and boot and shoe dealers. In 1909, the site of the Empire Theatre and former Grapes pub consisted of a tobacconist and pipe manufacturer, refreshment rooms, tobacconist and cigar importer, with the section at the junction with Lord Nelson Street a photographers, owned by Mr A. Saronie. The rooms above belonged to the Universal Recreation Company Billiard Saloon. In 1925, the whole block was demolished and its site extended over by a new theatre which retained the name the Empire and which remains one of the country's leading theatres.

One of the most famous of all Liverpool publicans was Mary Ellen Egerton. Her name is commemorated by the

THE VINES
A view of the premises in the 1920s when the manager was Thomas William Adamson, having little exterior difference from today. In common with other pubs of the town the cellars had passages leading down towards the River Mersey, reputedly used for smuggling.

(Above) Mary (Ma) Egerton entertaining visiting sailors. (Right) Ma Egerton with famous music-hall star Marie Lloyd.

45

public house, Ma Egertons (previously the Eagle Hotel) on the junction of Lord Nelson Street and Pudsey Street. Mary Egerton was known world wide, particularly in theatrical circles, although she rubbed shoulders with people from all walks of life, from sea captains to politicians, diplomats, sportsmen and the man in the street. She counted Marie Lloyd and Charlie Chaplin among her many personal friends. 'Peer or pauper they're all the same to me,' was one of her many phrases. She was so well loved in the theatre world that she became the only woman to become a non-theatrical member of their charity organisation, 'The Water Rats', with the honorary title of 'Lady Ratling'.

AMERICAN BAR (left)
Listed as 51-53 Lime Street and open to date. The photograph was taken in the 1890s when managed by Henry Winslade. Although this well-known city pub has long been known as the 'American Bar', few realise its correct name is the London Wine House Co. Ltd., so named about the time of the First World War, prior to which it was the Grey Horse and, earlier still, the North British Hotel in the 1860s and Midland Vaults during the 1880s.

CROWN HOTEL (below)
Listed as 43 Lime Street at the junction with Skelhorne Street. This view is from the 1890s, when the manager was William Crail, listed under the same name from c.1829, although during the last century it was called the Commercial before resuming its original name. The upstairs was in use as a billiards room. The adjoining dining rooms and restaurant, named 'Eves', traded under Henry Eves as Eves Central Hotel, until 1901.

COMMUTATION ROW
In the foreground is the Steble Fountain, a popular attraction for local children, particularly in the hot summer months. The Court House public house can be seen to the right of the fountain.

Born in an Irish market town, Belturbet, County Cavan in 1863, she travelled to London as a young woman and began to build up her circle of friends. She then moved to Liverpool in about 1890, acquiring the American Bar in Lime Street. On one of her frequent visits to London she was involved in the capture of Dr Hawley Harvey Crippen in 1910. Whilst in a London pub, she saw Crippen with a lady friend and recognised the jewellery the lady was wearing as belonging to Crippen's wife, Belle Elmore, who had been missing for some time. In a sensational case of the time, her important observation and other subsequent events, which included the first ever criminal suspect to be detained by the police through a radio receiver, led to Crippen being arrested and later hanged.

After the demolition of her pub on Lime Street, she acquired the Eagle, which was located at the other end of Pudsey Street at the junction of London Road. During the 1890s, the Eagle was listed as Bond's Hotel and earlier again Haye's Commercial Hotel.

A little higher up Lord Nelson Street stands the Lord Nelson Hotel which was originally a temperance hotel. There were ten other temperance hotels listed in Lord Nelson Street, some of which remain today in the form of small conventional hotels. Another pub of the street was the New Cross Keys, now a hotel named the Angel. Adjoining this hotel stands a larger building than the others, originally built in 1840 as the Owenite Hall Of Science, later in use as Concert Rooms and presently a furniture warehouse. Sadly, the remaining Georgian houses, numbers 27-33, although listed, have been in a state of decay for a number of years.

The continuation of Lime Street northward is Commutation Row where the Court House and Hare and Hounds stand.

THE CLOCK
Listed as 31 London Road, it was renamed the Dixie Dean Bar in 1986, after the city's most famous football player to grace Goodison Park. His record of scoring 60 goals in one season in the First Division is still unsurpassed. This pub dates back to the early years of the 19th century. It was named by the first licensee, a Mr Thomas Condliffe, whose brother James had a well-known clock-making business in nearby Fraser Street and it was to remain in the hands of his family for over fifty years.

London Road

THE LEGS OF MAN
The Legs Of Man, listed as 2 London Road and 1 Lime Street (originally 116 Lime Street), was probably built in the 1790s as a coaching inn, when it would have had stables at the rear. It was also a point for picking up mail from the old stage-coaches (probably taking over from the old Blue Bell). Its name is a bit of a mystery, as it appears to have no connection with the Isle of Man (although a number of pubs had this name, including one in Redcross Street listed as the Original Legs Of Man). The name may have originated from the Earls of Derby as they held a title 'Lord Of Man'. (In a police report from the 1890s, the Earl of Derby was listed as owning several pubs.)

London Road, the old 'road to Warrington' was only a narrow country track until 1760, when it was made passable for coaches. From that period, it rapidly became built up and was, by the turn of the 19th century, a densely populated part of the town, later to become one of the town's principal shopping thoroughfares. This remained until the 1960s when a gradual decline set in. At the time of writing, regeneration of the London Road vicinity has been implemented.

Three ancient inns of London Road were the Windmill, Gallows Mill and Blue Bell. The Windmill, which was close

to Norton Street, was a tiny thatched cottage. The Gallows Mill was close to Stafford Street and took its name from the gallows where Jacobite rebels were executed in 1715 from and the local windmills. The Blue Bell, close to Norton Street, was supposedly the first coaching inn of the road and, when it was demolished in the late 19th century, traces of the Siege of Liverpool during the Civil War of 1644 were discovered.

In the last century, there were terrible fights between the 'Orange & Green' (Protestants and Roman Catholics respectively). One such battle was recorded for the Liverpool Citizen in the 1880s by Charles Millward, who was in the Clock, on London Road.

'These turbulent and quarrelsome factions inevitably came into collision, and they frequently fought all along the lines of procession. The "yellows" usually hailed from Toxteth Park and the south end, and the "greens" turned out en masse from the unsavoury regions of Vauxhall and Scotland Roads and the far north. As the processions approached, or defiantly passed through the hostile districts the "enemy" would confront them in force, armed with any weapons they could procure, and most desperate fights would ensue. On many occasions men were killed and wounded on both sides, and there was a great destruction of property. Once upon a time I witnessed a terrible fight opposite Condliffes when a poor Irish man was shot dead; and some of the windows of the un-offending "Clock" were smashed. It was the first time I ever saw a man killed in a street fight.'

At the junction of Fraser Street, there was once a pub named the Saracens Head And Bell early in the 19th century. It was then renamed the Derby Arms until its closure in 1862. A new structure was built and opened in 1864. The premises had various uses over the years, part of

it was used as a club for a number of years and it was last in use in the 1980s as Trophy's night club. The building was demolished in 1994. A little lower down from the structure, stood a former well-known restaurant, Sampson And Barlows.

Prior to the 1960s, Lambert Street ran from London Road through to Islington, now terminating at Kempston Street. The section from here to Islington is now covered by modern industrial units. The Islington Tavern and a BH once stood here.

BROWNLOW HILL

To the south of London Road is the Copperas Hill/Brownlow Hill area, two ancient byways of Liverpool which were completely rural until the opening years of the 19th century, with windmills and a scattering of cottages lining the narrow country tracks. In the late 18th century, a copperas works opened on the then named Elliot Hill (copperas is crystalline ferrous sulphate used in the

An unnamed public house on the corner of Fairclough Lane and Lowndes Street, once part of the maze of streets that are now the site of the Royal Liverpool Teaching Hospital.

LORD WARDEN
A former WSV listed as 21 London Road, situated at the junction with Camden Street. It was named the Lord Warden in approximately 1880 and still has the same name. The photograph is from 1905 when the manager was Charles Inglis.

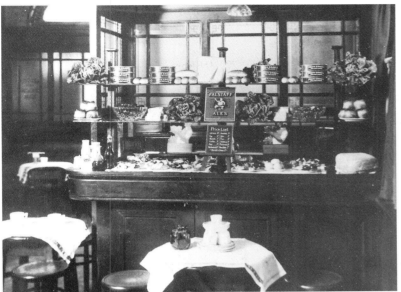

manufacture of fertilizers and inks). At this time, it changed its name to Copperas Hill and rapidly became built up. Running eastwards from the old Ranelagh Gardens in an irregular line, Copperas Hill was 619 yards long as far as Gill Street. It is hard to believe that Copperas Hill once contained nineteen pubs including Napoleon Vaults, Manchester Arms, London Tavern and the Swan With Two Necks.

The London Tavern was situated at the junction with Greek Street. It continued as a pub until demolition in the 1960s and was earlier named Pearson's Clock, probably after the 1892 licensee. The Swan With Two Necks was an early inn at the lower end of the hill at the junction of Hawke Street.

INTERIOR OF THE MONUMENT
A view of the pub's interior in 1926 showing the following price list:
Crab Salad 8d; Cheese Roll 3d; Egg Salad 6d; Roll 1d; Mussels 3d; Pies 4d; Cockles 3d; Salad 3d; Egg 3d; Pilchards 2¹/₂d; Sandwich 4d; Salad and Butter 1d; Biscuit and Cheese 1d.

THE MONUMENT (below)
Listed as 125 and 2 Audley Street (listed as 63 in the 1820s). This photograph is from the 1920s when the manager was William R. Kinghorn; the premises are currently closed.

PEMBROKE HOTEL (bottom right)
Listed as 66-68. Pembroke Place veers off London Road at Monument Place. This old pub was demolished approximately 20 years ago. The street on the corner of which it stood, Brownlow Street, now runs through the grounds of the University. The actual site of the pub is now part of the world renowned School of Tropical Medicine. The photograph from 1908 shows a butcher's shop belonging to William Read.

ROYAL (below)
Listed as 53-55 Pembroke Place, the Royal was located at the junction of Daulby Street and always referred to as the Daulby. This view is from the 1920s when the manager was James Pennycock. On the right can be seen a Dental Surgery, 57 Pembroke Place belonging to Alfred O. Calland; little would he realise whilst practising that, many years later, his premises would eventually become part of the site of Liverpool's Dental Hospital. The building shown with writing on the wall in Daulby Street was a carriage lamp makers, William Binnion and Son.

WINDSOR

A former WSV listed as 112 London Road and 1 Greek Street showing the now demolished three-storey houses of Greek Street. This view is from 1908 when the manager was John Evans. At the time of writing it is closed. (An old BH of London Road was listed as 112, although this closed as long ago as 1906 and was located almost facing this pub at the junction of Craven Street.)

HIGHLAND LADDIE

Listed as 158 London Road. Prior to 1862 it was named the Travellers Rest and then the Crown from the 1880s.

THE GRAPES

Looking from Monument Place, the building that now displays 'Windsor Fire Surrounds' was listed as a BH in the last century named the Grapes. About 1880 it was renamed George III until closure in the late 1950s. The building presently stands vacant and is situated at the junction of London Road and Moor Place. Further back is a tenement block of housing, known locally as the 'Bullring', which is undergoing renovation. On the left is a pub, Royal George, situated at the other junction of Pembroke Place and Moor Place, which pre-1860s was named the Exchange Vaults. The block on the left shown in use as a furniture shop was, in the last century, a hotel named the Somerset Hotel. The ongoing renovation scheme that is taking place in the London Road area caused this block to be demolished in 1993. A new building on this site has since been constructed consisting of shops and student accommodation.

STAFFORD ARMS

Listed as 82 Islington and at the junction with Stafford Street. The photograph is from the 1890s when the manager was Thomas Glover.

PRINCE OF WALES
This view from the 1970s shows very little difference to the exterior from the pub's early days, the main alteration was the centre door, which has since been closed and where there is now a round window was once a clock. The pub is closed at the time of writing. It was named the Green Man And Still throughout the last century and was numbered over the years as 56, 109, 205-207 and 225.

PRINCE OF WALES
Listed as 117 Kempston Street. A large pub at the junction of Moss Street, displaying the Original Prince of Wales Hotel, this may have been to distinguish it from the nearby Prince of Wales at the junction of London Road/Moss Street which, as earlier described, adopted this name after being known as the Green Man And Still for many years. The manager's name is also clearly displayed as James Vallelay in this photograph. The pub was later named the Prince Hotel. The site of this pub is open land on the fringe of a modern industrial estate.

No pubs remain on Copperas Hill. The Adelphi Restaurant, Fox & Goose and Brass Bar Vaults became the site of St Nicholas R.C. School in front of the pro-Cathedral. Between Gloucester Street and Brownlow Hill was a maze of court-ridden slums which were largely cleared in the 1930s, when the large complex of St Andrew's Gardens was constructed.

Hotham Street runs between London Road and Lord Nelson Street. A tiny section of the street also existed beyond Lime Street Station between Skelhorne Street and Copperas Hill until cleared for road improvements in the 1980s. The street originally led from London Road through to Copperas Hill before the railway station was extended. It is difficult to imagine nowadays that Skelhorne Street was just a narrow alley with the Boars Head at one junction.

Brownlow Hill leading eastward from the other side of Ranelagh Gardens also became a main thoroughfare, some 1,077 yards long, to Paddington. Before the massive upsurge in building, an ancient inn, the Black Bull, stood isolated close to the present site of Russell Street. Being a major road, it had its fair share of pubs although none remain. Although the construction of St Andrew's Gardens and, later, the R.C. Cathedral cleared some of the pubs, it was the early years of this century that saw massive closures. For example, by 1908, 24 pubs were listed on the road, whilst just four years later, 1912, this was reduced to sixteen.

On Gill Street, the Clock Tower Tavern belonged to Yates. Prior to demolition in the 1960s it was locally known as Clegg's. Yates, the Birkenhead brewery, had a small number of outlets in Liverpool with three in this vicinity; the Clock Tower Tavern, the Stags Head, Pembroke Place, and the Albion Vaults in Pembroke Street, which shut about the time of the First World War. Also on Gill Street was the Hide Market Inn.

At the foot of Brownlow Hill, Mount Pleasant veers off in an easterly direction, with its irregular line it then veers back in a northerly

ISLINGTON TAVERN
Formerly listed as 52 Lambert Street, at its junction with Islington, with the adjoining house a clothiers. When photographed in 1908, the manager was James H. Rowe. Closed during the 1940s, the actual site is now landscaped.

THE OLD FORT
The only public house left in Prescot Street. The photograph was taken in 1918 when the licensee was John Alfred Cann. The pawnbrokers are still trading.

COPPERAS HILL (below)
Copperas Hill once boasted nineteen public houses including the Globe Hotel, shown here on the corner of Russell Street. Photographed in 1955, the area was cleared soon after.

direction near the summit of Brownlow Hill. Originally Martindale Hill, it was the site of the Bowling Green Inn, owned by the father of William Roscoe, Liverpool's renowned 'Renaissance' man. The rural tranquillity was shattered when the expansion of the town engulfed the vicinity at the end of the eighteenth century. Two other ancient inns stood on Mount Pleasant: Union Tavern, located in the centre of the block, at the foot of the hill where Renshaw Street veers off to the left and the Ship Inn on the summit of Mount Pleasant at the junction of Brownlow Hill and facing the town's workhouse, which was built in the 18th century on the outskirts of the town. The workhouse is now the site of the R.C. Cathedral. The inn was later renamed William IV and closed in approximately 1880.

Mount Pleasant built up with fine Georgian town houses for the rich merchants who had begun their exodus from the crowded lower part of the town. From the mid-19th century, many of the Georgian town houses began to be converted into temperance and later conventional hotels. One of the earliest was the Cambridge House Temperance Hotel, listed as 50 in the 1870s, the building still remaining, whilst the adjoining 52-54 was named the Commercial and Temperance Hotel, listed to William Hunt in the 1890s, more recently listed as Hunt's Hotel. The building is currently in private use.

The drinking establishment half way up Mount Pleasant

NAPOLEON VAULTS
Formerly listed as 29 Copperas Hill at the junction of Hilbre Street. This 1909 photograph, taken when the manager was John McMaddy, shows a street sign 'Hilbre Street Late Hill Street'. The premises closed the following year and were later in use as cocoa rooms. The site of this pub is presently a car park.

has long been known as the Irish Centre. This listed building was originally built in 1815-16 as a Subscription Assembly Room for the Wellington Club. All the property on the lower section of the north side of Mount Pleasant was demolished in the early 1970s for a multi-storey car park.

THE GOAT
Listed as 42 St Andrew Street. It was photographed in 1908 when the licensee was Margaret K. Baker, with a group of men outside – a normal practice of bygone days when men would gather outside pubs wishing they could afford a pint. Pre-1860s it was known as Porter Butt. It was situated at the junction of St Andrew Street and Bronte Street. One of seven former pubs of St Andrew Street pre-1930s. It closed during the 1920s when it was part of a huge demolition programme for the construction of St Andrew's Gardens.`

WARREN
Listed as 44 Warren Street. A former BH earlier named the Dive and, pre-1880s, the Diving Bell. It featured the cellar of a dwelling house that was in use as a pub in the 1880s when the manager was John Edwardson. It lost its licence in 1910. Warren Street formerly led between Hawke Street and Russell Street when the old property existed. The street has since been renamed Royal Mail Street and leads to the comparatively new Royal Mail sorting office.

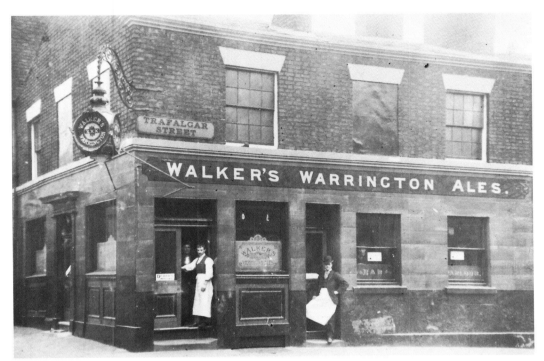

OLD RED HOUSE
This old pub clearly displays the name Trafalgar Street, although the premises were listed as 56 Trowbridge Street. The street once contained court property surrounding the old slaughterhouse that also stood on the street. At present, post-Second World War housing lines Trowbridge Street adjacent to St. Andrew's Gardens. The pub closed in 1914. The photograph is from the 1890s when the manager was James Hodgson.

DRAGON VAULTS
Listed as 163-165 Brownlow Hill, formerly at the junction of Brownlow Street. The street vanished into the site of the University and the pub was demolished in the 1960s. The photograph is from the 1920s when the manageress was Mrs Jessie Laycock.

AERIAL VIEW
Mount Pleasant in 1959. The Shaftesbury Hotel on the right was also first listed as a temperance hotel in the 1870s.

WHITE STAR VAULTS
Formerly listed as 1 Clarence Street at the junction of Brownlow Hill, clearly displaying its name in the 1920s when the manager was John Nathan Albert. The pub was demolished in the 1960s prior to which it was locally referred to as Macs and, earlier, the White Cunard. Its site is presently landscaping, fronting the University.

REGENT
This view from 1936 features a shop listed as 46 Mount Pleasant, housing three different businesses – tobacconist, watch repairer and barber shop. The sign indicates that Smith's Regent Hotel was to take over. Extensive alterations and refacing of the building then occurred. The hotel opened in 1939 as Smith's Regent Hotel until approximately 1970 and is now the Regent Hotel.

WHITE HORSE
Listed as 26 and 21 Hartford Street. A former WSV, this pub closed in the 1930s. Its site is now part of the car park. Photographed in the 1890s when the manager was Edmund Ayres.

CLARENCE HOUSE
Listed as 22 Pleasant Street at the junction of Clarence Street. This view is from the 1920s when the manager was Joseph Hughes. It closed as a PH in the 1930s. It was earlier known as Rodney Hotel and, during the 19th century, Artist Vaults. In the 1980s, it reopened as licensed premises named Bonaparte's.

BEEHIVE
Listed as 14 Mount Pleasant it remains open to date and the present exterior has not altered a great deal this century.

NEW CROWN HOTEL
Listed as 2-6 Brownlow Hill at the juction with a narrow alley named Chapel Lane, a large imposing pub with Blezards name displayed on the window. On the extreme left, just visible, is the Nook PH listed as 12, at the junction of Mary Ann Street.

Queen Square

QUEEN SQUARE (1920)

The destruction that took place in the area during the 1960s transformed the area of Queen Square and Williamson Square beyond recognition. Queen Square has now been obliterated and, although Williamson Square still stands, it can barely be recognised from the quaint quarter of the 1960s.

In St Johns Lane, in the 1960s, the former Victoria Hotel stood at the junction with Roe Street (presently part of a widened road). Further down stood the Mona PH, at the junction of Tryon Street. One building lower down, formerly the Pearl Assurance Building, built in approximately 1901, was surprisingly one of the very few structures that managed to escape the mass demolition of

the area, having various uses over the years including a night club during the 1980s. After being empty for a number of years, the ground floor recently opened as a pub, Casper's Inn. St John's Lane is a prime example of the way the numbering of the city centre streets altered over the years; the Victoria Hotel, for example, was listed as follows: 1881 (Victoria Vaults) no. 40, 1891 (Victoria Vaults) no. 24, 1898 (Victoria Hotel) no. 38, 1901 (Victoria Hotel) no. 24, 1905 (Victoria Hotel) no. 21.

Basnett Street formerly contained seven public houses which included the Rainbow Hotel, listed as 44. For some 30 years between 1850 and 1880, this well-patronised hotel was one of the town's excellent hostelries, owned by a Mr Lawton, a well-loved chef. He reputedly kept the best Irish whiskey outside of Ireland, of which apparently

THE GRAPES (above)
An old Higsons house, the Grapes, was next to the last remaining shop of the block on Upper Dawson Street, the Army Stores. The pub was listed as 18 Upper Dawson Street and originally named the 'Three Tuns', it was renamed the Grapes during the 1860s which it remained until closure in 1964; it was locally known as 'Dolly's', probably after Dorothy Stephenson, a former manageress.

QUEEN SQUARE
A lone figure walks amongst the mass demolition in what looks like a scene from the last war, but this was 1964 not 1944. The site of the market to the right (just shown) was cleared and the remainder of the property is in an advanced stage of demolition. The clock tower of the Municipal Building can be seen in the distance. The building in the centre, which appears the least affected by demolition, was at one time a pub named the Preston Tavern, at the junction of Upper Dawson Street.

only Mr Lawton knew the brand and he never sold any of it to be taken off the premises. Towards the end of his lease he left to run another pub, the Bee, in the nearby Queen Square, taking the majority of his old customers with him. The Rainbow then rapidly declined, becoming an 'ordinary' public house described by Charles Millward in 1888:

> '*Once upon a time, before betting clubs and similar nuisances were invented, the Rainbow Hotel, at the corner of Basnett Street and Houghton Street, was a thriving and well-patronised hostelry. When I passed it a few weeks ago the house appeared to have been merged into an ordinary public and the hotel part had evidently become a haunt for a very low class of the "genus" betting men. Gentlemen to whom honest labour has long been an unknown quantity, men who "spin not, neither do they toil", were hurrying in and out of the place, and small groups of them held noisy altercation at the door, and kept up a ceaseless din at the street corner. It was more like an edifying scene, and it appeared to me more like a gathering of the scum of the city than an assemblage at a house which was once a respectable and well-conducted hotel. When I last saw it I was glad to get away from it.*'

DUCK HOUSE
Once a very well-known pub listed at 14 Upper Dawson Street. It was named in approximately 1845, prior to that it was the Butcher's Arms and then the Old Stores. The pub remained trading until the mass demolition of the area in the 1960s. This view is from the 1920s when the licensee was James Walsh.

MAGIC CLOCK
Listed as 7 Roe Street, this old pub which stood close to Queen Square remained until the 1970s when, like so many more, it was converted to dust and rubble. The manager at this time was John Murray Shergold. During the last century, it was named the Champion.

From a quaint, early 19th-century town square, it was becoming a bustling area by the 1850s. During the 1880s it became the centre of vice and crime until, during the late 1890s, the area rapidly changed once more. The Rainbow stood at the junction of Basnett Street/Houghton Street, the site becoming part of the large department store, George Henry Lee, which was extended over the former pub in 1897. Incidentally, after the death of Mr Lawton, the secret of the famous old Irish whiskey was not passed on to his successor, a Mr Penn, at the Bee. Basnett Street still stands between Church Street and Williamson Square and is now a pedestrian area no longer containing any pubs.

The Belmont was formerly one of 12 pubs on Houghton Street, which was 117 yards long. It was probably rebuilt around 1862 as, prior to the 1860s, it was named the Crown And Grapes. The pub's name is taken from Shakespeare's 'Merchant of Venice'. In the play, the heroine's house was named 'Belmont'. Stained glass panels

QUEEN SQUARE
This view of the bustling Queen Square was photographed from the Stork Hotel just after the war. The Royal Court Theatre shown on the rear left is the only building remaining today. I think even the planners may now realise their mistake, allowing many quaint and important parts of the city such as this to be destroyed during the 1960s and '70s. Imagine the old fruit market that once thrived in the Queen Square vicinity in full bloom today. Tourists as well as local people would be able to stroll around the cobbled area where a strong healthy aroma once filled the air.

separating the saloon and lounge bars depicted scenes from the play and, I was informed by Ann Callan, the daughter of a former licensee, Peter Callan, that a large tiled mural of Shylock (villain in the play) hung upside down in the pub creating much interest.

The pub was the last to be demolished on Houghton Street in May, 1964. Ironically, during the same week 'The Merchant of Venice' was being performed in the nearby Royal Court Theatre. Actress Jean Kent and other members of the cast together with members from the Playhouse Theatre were amongst a packed crowd on the last night, who presented a scroll to Peter Callan describing him as 'The noblest publican of them all', parodying the Shakespearean quotation from 'Julius Caesar'. For years the pub was the haunt of some of Britain's top stage and screen stars. Peter Callan was the licensee from 1951-64 and, at the time of writing, is in his 90s and has fond memories from his days as licensee. On the last night of opening he stated:

'This is the greatest night in the Belmont's history. It's really wonderful to see so many old friends here. It's terribly sad we have to close, but I suppose we must make way for progress.

We have always been known as the show-biz pub - a place where the ordinary man in the street could rub shoulders and have a chat with the top stars. But, alas, all good things have to come to an end. Tomorrow we will just be the pub with no beer.'

Eagle Tavern was known for many years as O'Neills, like most nicknames taken from the name of a former manager. O'Neill himself was a remarkable man. Born in Ireland in 1812, like many of his fellow country men he left Ireland as a young man to seek work in England. He first worked in a cotton mill in Manchester. After losing this job, he turned up penniless in St Helens and it was here that he met his future wife who was working as a cook to a gentleman.

After acquiring a job in St Helens and having a small

SHAKESPEARE
Listed as 8 Williamson Square, this is at the junction of the Square and Dawson Street. It has been on this site since the 1840s and has retained the same name except for a brief period in the 1870s when named Red House Hotel: a nearby pub was named the Original Shakespeare Tavern. This view of the pub with the manager's name J. H. W. Cooper clearly displayed on the window is from 1908 (J. H. W. standing for John Henry Worsley). Before the demolition of the old property on Dawson Street (the street remains, presently a widened thoroughfare), facing the pub at the junction with Marble Street stood the Globe Tavern PH, and a little lower towards Whitechapel was a PH named the British Queen.

QUEEN SQUARE VICINITY
This 1964 view illustrates the actual location of Queen Square to the left of the Royal Court Theatre and, although trade is continuing, demolition is already in progress. The block (centre left) where the Magic Clock can be seen was on Roe Street and stood for nearly ten more years together with the Stock Hotel in the background, whilst the large empty area was once the market and adjacent property.

amount of savings, they decided to try their prospects in Liverpool. They first succeeded in opening up a bowling alley in Houghton Street, although John O'Neill's ambition was to make billiard tables. Through the success of the bowling alley, enough money was made to acquire the Eagle PH in the same street. Once established, O'Neill soon had a billiard table built in the pub, this supposedly being the first pub in Liverpool to house one. He then converted his bowling alley into a billiard hall which contained eight tables. John O'Neill died in 1880 - from being a poor Irish immigrant he ended his days a wealthy man and the founder of billiard table manufacturing in Liverpool.

The Star, in Williamson Square, was a notorious fighting house, particularly during the 1840s when it was kept by a well-known publican-cum-boxer named James (Jemm) Ward. Nightly brawls were commonplace in such pubs as the Star, keeping the landlords (many of whom were former boxers) in plenty of practise. This old brawling house closed down in the late 1850s to be replaced by a music hall of the same name. Once converted into a music hall it virtually

QUEEN SQUARE
This night view from the Square to Gt. Charlotte Street was taken in 1957. The Stork Hotel is partly shown on the right, whilst the pub lit up displaying 'Bents' sign was the Roebuck, listed at 14 Gt. Charlotte Street and 15 Hood Street (later renamed Tryon Street).

had four public houses situated within the hall. A gin shop on the left, public bar in the centre, an oyster bar selling drinks on the right and the basement known as the Dive. In 1903, on the renewal of the theatrical licence, the licensee undertook to allow the licence of the Dive in the basement to lapse and it closed in the same year. In 1912, after reconstruction, where an adjoining warehouse was taken over, the old Star Music Hall was then renamed the Playhouse Theatre which remains to date. The following police report from 1892 stated:

> 'The licensee of this house was cautioned at the last annual licensing sessions for permitting the resort of prostitutes. This year the police have constantly visited the house, and have found prostitutes there on many occasions. These women are generally found in the public house portion of the premises only, the music hall being fairly well conducted for a place of entertainment of the class.'

After the closure of the Star, Jemm Ward took over the nearby York Hotel, which stood at the junction of Williamson Square and Tarleton Street. It was listed as 30 Tarleton Street and 25 Williamson Square and was earlier named the Tarleton Hotel. Although a more desirable establishment than the old Star, fighting nevertheless continued but was mainly confined to a 'boxing room'.

The hotel was also noted for other sporting events. During Grand National week, the hotel would be booked solid with the nightly singing rooms packed to capacity. Many famous and local dignitaries frequented the York, such as Sir John Gerrard and other family members from Croxteth Hall. On one occasion during Grand National week, Sir John and his party were accompanied by Prince Louis Napoleon. At the request of the Prince, he and his distinguished party were entertained in the boxing room. A fight took place between Jemm Ward and Matt Robinson,

CARNARVON CASTLE
Listed as 5 Tarleton Street which is now a pedestrian area between Williamson Square and Church Street. It is the only one remaining of eight pubs that stood in the Street. There has been a considerable change to the facade of this pub. The view is from 1944 when managed by Brian James Parry. In the 1880s, Charles Millward described this pub as 'one of the neatest and snuggest little "publics" in all the city'.

who was the manager of the nearby Grecian Saloon PH. Afterwards, the Prince himself sparred with Jemm who, for obvious reasons, was careful not to hit the Prince too hard!

The Grecian Saloon was another old brawling pub, situated facing the Theatre Royal stage door in Murray Street, later renamed Brythen Street. Numerous 'fisticuffs' would have taken place in this pub, especially if the entertainment at the theatre was disliked by the crowd. From the 1860s, the pub was named the Falstaff and, from the 1890s, renamed Quinn's, a Greenall Whitley house. This was located adjoining the Old Royal. A 1892 police report stated:

OLD ROYAL (1890s)
Listed as 2 Brythen Street this was at the junction of Upper Dawson Street. Many pubs had little change to their exterior over the years, whilst others such as this, as can be seen when compared to the 1920s view, altered enormously. This photograph was taken in the 1890s when the manager was Richard Lloyd.

OLD ROYAL (1920s)
This view is from the 1920s when the manager was Jonathan Nixon. The pub adjoining this was Quinn's.

'At the last annual licensing sessions the licensee gave an undertaking to the bench not to serve prostitutes. This promise the licensee has fairly conformed to.'

I wonder if the two police officers deployed on the amusing incident that occurred in Williamson Street on the 10th August, 1877, were as conscientious?:

'Inspector Rogerson reported that about 8.50 a.m. on Friday, 10th August he with police constable 276 Bulman visited the house 28 Williamson Street kept by Mary Barton who is licensed to sell foreign wines & etc., and found in bed upstairs a man whom she stated was her manager, and in answer to Inspector she stated she was not married. Inspector informed her that from what he then saw he had reason to believe that she and the man who she stated was her manager, had been sleeping together and that he would make a report of the matter for the information of the licensing magistrates. She replied "I have nothing to say I cannot help it".'

I cannot trace 28 Williamson Street as a BH in any directories, although the Richmond Arms, 32, may have taken the premises over during in the last century.

The Conway Castle closed in 1986. The building is presently in use as a store trading under the name of Superdrug. Listed as 23 Tarleton Street, the pub was acquired by Yates Brothers, in 1929, and converted into one of their wine lodges. The premises were rebuilt incorporating part of the original name by naming the lounge 'Conway Lounge'. An article written at the time reporting the reconstruction of the building reports:

'The rebuilding took place by Joseph Yates and Company (the building division of Yates Bros. & Co.). A discovery of great importance was made in the person of Jim Yates who was found working amongst the labourers on the site! Jim Yates, nephew of Peter Yates, and twin brother of Joe, was later to manage Bolton Wine Lodge and was subsequently moved to Blackpool as assistant to his brother Joe. He died in 1963.'

During the rebuilding, a note by Sam Bradbury for Peter Yates read as follows:

'You will observe that we are still pouring out the money for the Conway Castle. It appears to me that the scheme is altogether too elaborate and quite unnecessary for our class of business. It will take some years before we get our money back, if ever. I suppose time will show, but my opinion is that all these up-to-date machines, lifts, refrigerators, washing machines, neon signs etc. etc. were not necessary. The business was not built up on these lines. I remember the time when we built up tea chests and champagne cases for counters.'

The note is endorsed,

'I quite agree. Put the brake on. P.Y.'

Back in Victorian Liverpool there was another famous pub of Tarleton Street, Eureka, described by Charles Millward:

'There were few licensed houses in the town so well known during the last twenty five years as Mrs White's. I am not sure that it had any other name but if it had, I certainly never heard of it. As a dinner, tea and supper house, Mrs White's had no superior, whilst as for its pies they were also as widely known as St George's Hall, and quite as much admired, although of course, in a different sort of way.'

As stated elsewhere, older generations today will argue that beers and spirits are not as strong as in their day - something that has, and probably will continue to occur, as the following from 1890 suggests:

'It also achieved a high reputation for the excellence of its liquor, which fact, combined with its other more solid attractions, proved irresistible to the jolly old boys of twenty years ago. They did not care a lot for the gorgeous fittings and luxurious upholstery. Not they! But they soon found out a house where good beverages and food were dispensed and flocked there accordingly. And couldn't those "old boys" do justice to the refreshments, either liquid or solid, set before them! Why, we living in this jubilee age are simply not in it at all! Their capacity for consuming alcoholic beverages in particular was sufficient to extort admiration and astonishment from the meek and mild toppers of today. I was talking recently with a fine old crusted specimen of a "bon vivant" aged 84 and he told me that nothing struck him so forcibly as the change that has come over the drinking habits of the community. Twenty five or thirty years ago he said, it was a very unusual thing for a man to order a glass of beer in the parlour of a first-class tavern or hotel. In fact, his companions would have regarded him with something akin to contempt if he did so. Glasses, not half-glasses, of brandy or whisky were the orders most frequently given in those bibulous times, and they were emptied and replenished at a rate suggestive of very hard heads and strong stomachs being the property of the consumers.'

The modern 'plastic' pub, so often complained about nowadays by traditionalists, is also nothing new as the following suggests:

'If ever I have witnessed a transformation scene out of a pantomime, I believe it is the gorgeous sight which met my eyes a few evenings ago, when I visited the premises once known as Mrs White's. Not a single vestige of its former self remains. The floor has been made almost level with the pavement, the bow-window has been replaced by a fine sheet

COMPTON HOUSE, Church Street
Originally, Compton House opened in 1832 in Church Street as a drapers shop, eventually extending to take in the whole block between Basnett Street and Tarleton Street; this was destroyed by fire and the block rebuilt in 1867. The Compton Hotel was a part of this block listed as 41 in the 1870s, then, by the 1880s had expanded and was listed 39, 41, 43. Thereafter it remained a well-known city centre hotel until closure in 1926. From approximately 1930 Marks and Spencer occupied a portion of the former hotel, expanding to take most of the block.

of plate glass, bordered with tasteful examples of the glass stainers' art. The interior is sumptuously fitted with mahogany counters, mirrors, and luxurious fixtures, while over the window I noticed "The Eureka" shine forth in all the glory of large gold letters.'

The article finishes:

'I myself was simply astonished at the change that had been effected in two or three months, but I wonder what would be the state of mind of one of the "old boys" who used to frequent the house a quarter of a century ago, if he could only return to the scene of his revelry once more, and gaze on the wealth of decoration which would greet his eyes as he entered "The Eureka"'.

Incidentally, Mrs White's was named the Cheshire Cheese and its replacement just described appears to have been a 'monster' gin palace of its era but, like so many other pubs of the town, this too closed about the time of the First World War. It did open for a short period in the 1920s, as Dunger's Grill, but closed during the same decade. The premises were formerly directly facing the Conway Castle, now the site of a large department store.

In the section of Great Charlotte Street that led from Whitechapel to Queen Square was the Spanish House, a former Bents house situated at the junction of Whitechapel/Gt. Charlotte Street. It was earlier named the Victoria and originally listed as the Old Spanish Wine House, 21 Old Haymarket. Most of Gt. Charlotte Street/Queen Square is presently the site of a car park.

Not too far from Queen Square is another of the city's famous squares, Clayton Square. This survived longer than Queen Square and was only demolished in the 1980s and rebuilt as a new shopping precinct. It was named after an old Liverpool family, the Claytons. Originally a quiet retreat within the town until approximately 1822, when Elliot Street was formed and cut through to Lime Street, it then became a bustling quarter of the town. Many of the houses of merchants who lived in the Square were then converted into hotels and offices as the former inhabitants moved to quieter pastures. The Square once had seven hotels: Bull Hotel, Castle Hotel, Dolphin Hotel, Neptune Hotel, Union Hotel, Clayton Hotel and the Feathers Hotel.

Tom McInerney, the licensee of the Feathers Hotel, was a respected victualler of his time after his previous career as

VINE HOTEL
A neat, tiled exterior to this pub listed as 11-13 Gt. Charlotte Street and having an earlier name, the Grapes. Photographed in 1908 when the manager was William Lloyd.

a wrestler, boxer and athlete. Born in Ireland, he emigrated to America when only fifteen, later settling in Liverpool, where he was frequently involved in both wrestling and boxing matches. Probably his most well-known wrestling match was against the famous Russian, Georg Hackensmidt, who was World Champion for fourteen years. Tom McInerney won £2,000 in a three-round challenge bout against him and he was reputedly to have said of him, 'he was the strongest man ever born'. Tom McInerney died in 1934.

In Victorian Liverpool, with limited entertainment, many clubs sprang up which were attached to pubs and hotels. One such club was formed in the Feathers, when a number of gentlemen patronising the hotel decided, as a joke, to thrust a pair of scissors, material and some cotton into one of their friend's silk hat. The victim of this prank, unaware of his predicament, left the premises with a 'train' of material etc. in tow. Upon discovering his misfortune and not seeing the funny side of it, he returned to the hotel in an angry and threatening mood. However, on being told he could be charged with walking off the premises with the hotel's property, he eventually accepted the joke and it simply ended as a happy lark.

It was this amusing, insignificant incident that led directly to the forming of the 'Bobbin and Scissor Club', which quite rapidly boasted amongst its members many of the town's leading citizens. Another unusual club existed in a pub named the Clarendon in South John Street and this description of it was given by Charles Millward in 1888:

'A striking feature about the Clarendon at this time was a bogus club, which held its meetings there whenever it suited its members to do so. It was called the "Diabolicals", and well deserved the name, but was productive of more fun than anything of the sort I have ever seen or read of. The principal objects of this precious society, as announced with unblushing effrontery by the secretary or chairman, were first "the enrolment of new members" and second, the

GARRICK
Formerly listed as 19 Gt. Charlotte Street. Previously named the Garricks Head. The name over the window reads 'Mersey Brewery', which refers to the former Cains Brewery in Upper Stanhope Street, whilst the pub's name was engraved over the accommodation. Photographed from 1908 when the manager was George Hopkins.

An unnamed public house in the Old Hay Market in 1828. The site is now the entrance to the Mersey Tunnel.

"obtaining of cheap drinks", i.e., drinks paid for by somebody else. This being, of course, any unlucky person who consented to join the club, the entrance fee being glasses round for the company!'

Although these two 'clubs' are relics of a bygone age, surprisingly one existed as late as 1991 of which I was a member. Devised by John E. Puddifer of Bootle purely as a joke, he listed 30 regulars of Manchester Street Wine Lodge as the 'Whingeing Wino's Club', each being issued with a scroll and number written by John.

Off Clayton Square stood the narrow Cases Street which, since the demolition of Clayton Square, remains only as a short entrance into the new development from Ranelagh Street, yet still has two pubs remaining on this small section.

In the nearby Elliot Street, close to the pub named the Villiers, was a pub with the unusual name of Number Ten (its street number) and for a number of years before the First World War listed as Creedon's. Before the construction of the nearby cinema at the junction of Back Lime Street stood a pub named the Niagara Vaults.

CENTRAL
Listed as 29-31 Ranelagh Street. It is a highly decorative pub. Its full name is the Central Commercial Hotel, so named since 1887 having previously known as the Albion Hotel. The facade carries two dates, one of 1887 when renamed, and a mysterious 1675. This photograph is from the 1920s when the manager was Alfred C. Thorley.

71

MIDLAND

Listed as 25-27 Ranelagh Street and 21 Cases
Street and still a thriving pub. This view is
from before the First World War when the
manager was William Thomas. The building
itself was constructed in the early 19th
century, having various commercial uses
until approximately 1870 when it became a
public house. The adjoining shop shown on
Cases Street was listed as 19 to Nelly Hamill,
Hairdresser and is currently a fashion
clothes shop.

QUEEN SQUARE MAP (below)

*'Study of the Queen Square area reveals some
very ugly facts. Within a radius of 100 yards
from St John's Market are 68 drinking places,
and many of them so altered since obtaining
their licences, that they are the same as two, and
in some instances three public houses. A perusal
of this map will show unmistakably how the
magistrates of the borough are defied by the
public-house interest in Liverpool. The state of
Williamson Square on the one side of the district
marked on the map, and Lime Street on the
other, is simply a disgrace to the authorities of
the town.'* (1875)

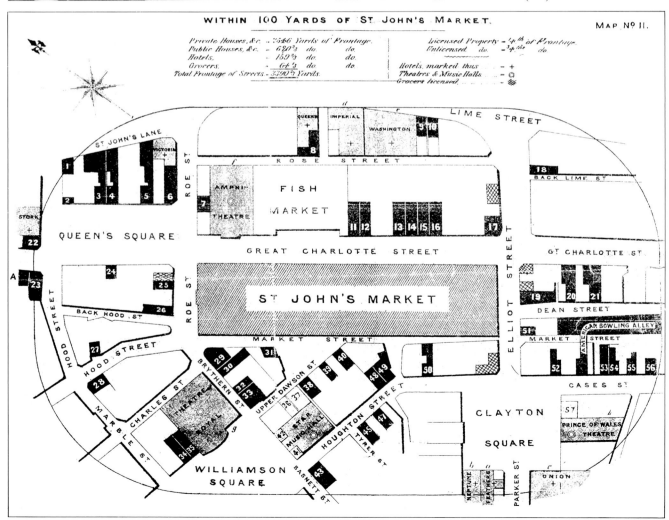

Liverpool 1

MANN ISLAND (c.1895)

This chapter covers the southern vicinity of the city centre and south as far as the former boundary of the old town (Parliament Street). All are Liverpool 1 with a few exceptions as stated.

In the 18th and 19th centuries, the vicinity of the Old Dock area (the present Canning Place) was known as 'Sailor Town' and contained numerous pubs, lodging houses and seedy brothels that catered for the enormous number of seamen who frequented the area, making it a most notorious quarter of the town. Before the docks became isolated from the general public, pubs, together with court property where dockers would have lived, once stood on the dock estate.

The immediate area south of the present Pier Head was originally named Nova Scotia, or New Scotland, which, in the early 18th century, contained houses tenanted by sea captains and merchants and was probably named by sailors trading between the port and Nova Scotia. In 1767 work

commenced on George's Dock and one of the tenants of Nova Scotia was John Mann, an Oil Stone Dealer and Walking Stick Maker (the former apparently a very lucrative business). During the four years of construction of the new dock, John Mann, surveying the work, was delighted that Nova Scotia would become an 'Island' and apparently never ceased to impress upon his neighbours that he would shortly be living on an 'Island'. When George's Dock opened in 1771, land between it and the dry dock had in fact become an artificial island and was jocularly referred to as 'Mann's Island'. To the delight of John Mann, the common council officially adopted the name Mann Island as an appellation for part of Nova Scotia and, although George's Dock closed in 1900 to be replaced by the present Pier Head, Mann Island and Nova Scotia remain to the present day.

In Nova Scotia stood a pub named the Dickey Sam Inn, one of two so named in this vicinity. During the days of the old sailing ships, 'Liverpudlians' were known as 'Dickey

GEORGES DOCK PASSAGE
Mann Island is on the left. The public house on the left offered sailors a final chance for a quiet drink before their ship left for the open river.

MANN ISLAND (1830)

Sams', although a true 'Dickey Sam' was supposed to be born on Mann Island. When a ship was outward bound from the George's Dock it had to pass slowly through a 'gutter' hauled by rope; it was here where the pub stood. Many a sailor would have jumped ashore for a last drink,

then joined the ship further down the 'cut'. This 'cut' was named Georges Dock Passage and five other pubs once stood here (Wexford Tavern, Conway Castle, West Country Tavern and two PHs not numbered).

Another story concerning the origin of 'Dickey Sam' is that during the time of Press Gangs, they descended on Mann Island and seized some twenty men. When these involuntary recruits were marshalled on deck to get their names entered into the ship's book, the warrant officer demanded of one of them his name. He answered 'Dickey Sam', the second man also answered 'Dickey Sam' and so on until up to twenty had answered the same name. The angry warrant officer was about to order a lashing for the men when a lieutenant, well versed in the nature of Mann Island, explained that every occupant of that island was named Richard Samuel, hence Dickey Sam.

GOREE PIAZZA

A magnificent view of the old Goree Piazza warehouses situated in the centre of the picture looking north. Behind them you can see the warehouses of the Strand, where the White Star Building (1898) towers over them at the junction of James Street. On the left is the former impressive Overhead Railway.

A View of OLD HOUSES. South side James's St. 1828.

OLD HOUSE, James Street (1828)

It is known that there was a Richard Samuel listed as a victualler on Mann Island and, during the 1840s, a ship named the Dickey Sam came to grief on the north shore and its cargo which included tobacco and rum was apparently plundered by locals.

Numerous pubs were built as Liverpool rapidly expanded from the first dock in 1715, through turbulent and exciting times. The early ship owners and merchants of the town grew wealthy on the spoils accumulated by the slave trade, so much so that they fought tooth and nail against its abolition, fearing their business and port would be ruined. After the abolition quite the reverse happened, trade was opened up with China and rapidly expanded throughout the world, creating more and larger docks.

However, as the merchants and ship owners flourished, at the other end of the ladder squalor and poverty also thrived. The Canning Place/Mann Island vicinity became a most squalid corner of the town during the late 18th and early 19th centuries as the merchants found pastures new. It was during these times another blemish in Liverpool's turbulent history occurred, that of the press gangs roaming the streets, seizing men by force for the Peninsular Wars; often the last 'hiding place' for hunted men were the cellars of houses and pubs in this area. The majority of men seized by the press gangs were never heard of again and, for sailors lucky enough to survive long hard trips at sea, once in Liverpool they would rarely get past the pubs and taverns around the docks; the footpads and hooligans would see to that. A common early morning occurrence was the fishing of a drunken, battered body of a sailor, minus his wages, out of the dock.

TRAWLER
Listed as 12 Strand Street, this pub previously had the name the Globe early this century but changed its name in approximately 1912 when the licensee was Hugh Kennedy. It was the last pub on the street to be demolished.

JAMAICA VAULTS
The section of the 'Dock Road' south from James Street is named Strand Street, now a widened throroughfare. This pub was listed as 3 & 4 Strand Street near the junction of Sea Brow, one of nearly 40 pubs that were situated here, it closed in the late 1950s.

A rare, supposedly true story concerning a man who survived the press gangs was as follows:

'A local block maker named William McCoid who lived on Mann Island, having just been married, left the church for a supply of beer at a local tavern. To the amazement of guests and the consternation of his bride he did not return. After a lapse of several weeks a letter was received stating he had been impressed and was on board a frigate sailing to foreign parts. After three years, the frigate, which had taken part in several actions, and had captured a number of valuable prizes arrived home and was paid off. McCoid, flush with his wages and prize money, at once took a coach home. The coach was stopped by armed men, a couple seized the leaders whilst the others surrounded the vehicle and called on the passengers to alight. Needless to say, it was the dreaded press gang. McCoid was at once seized, his pleas ignored with the need of the country for men so desperate and, within a few days McCoid was again at sea within a king's ship. Four years passed before he again returned, this time in safety and at long last was reunited with his bride. McCoid apparently lived to a ripe old age.'

THE CUSTOM HOUSE HOTEL
The Custom House, a magnificent classical building, and its immediate neighbourhood, was almost totally destroyed by enemy bombing. The Custom House Hotel, named after its nearby landmark is just one of the many buildings left as a shell.

Facing Mann Island is James Street, one of the town's older streets. On the north side of the street junction of the Strand stands Albion House, erected in 1898. A listed building, formerly the White Star building, it was one of the first of the giant office blocks built in the city and replaced a number of pubs, including the Golden Salmon, earlier Hope Tavern. During the 1840s the latter was split into two separate trades, a public house and eating house. The owner of both was a Mr Haddrall, a victualler and fish curer, which was quite a combination, as a thirst would be in order after a nice meal of salmon! It was also a favourite haunt of sea captains and officers mainly trading with the west coast of Africa and, with fortunes to make in those days, pubs such as the Golden Salmon were literally goldmines for their owners. As always, however, the premises were eventually taken over and converted to a hotel named the Mona, listed as 16. The rear of these premises was listed in the 1870s as a British & Foreign Wine Dealers; this was destroyed during the war and the rebuilt premises were named the Liverpool in 1984 after H.M.S. Liverpool, commissioned in 1982 as the seventh ship to bear the name.

A little higher stood Dodd's Hotel which, prior to its demolition late in the last century, was generally thought to be the town's oldest licensed premises. It was named the Eastham Packet House in the 1840s and in the 1820s named the Eastham And Chester Packet House, when the licensee was Dod Betha, probably taking the name Dodd's from this licensee. In the 18th century and early 19th century, it was also a booking point for passengers travelling to Eastham and Chester. Late in the last century, the pub was renamed from Dodd's to the Grapes and closed about the time of the First World War. The premises were probably rebuilt at that time as its name was once again listed as Dodd's until destroyed during the Second World War.

Facing Albion House is the Harbour Vaults, later renamed the Mersey Tunnel Vaults (pre-1860s listed as Birkenhead & Cheshire Hotel). This closed around the time of the First World War and its site (rebuilt) later became a seamen's mission, then a hotel. In the late 1980s and early 1990s the premises became vacant once again and, at the time of writing, has reopened as a pub named Coopers.

Further up James Street was a pub named the Grey Horse, listed in the 1820s as 65 before numerical changes. It was so named after a magnificent stuffed horse that dominated the bar, which apparently made more money for the licensee than when it was alive! It was thought to have been removed later to Lime Street to a pub also named the Grey Horse, where it was once again exhibited. I presume this was its last residence, as its whereabouts after here is unknown. The only other pub remaining on James Street is the Queens Hotel (rebuilt), standing at the junction of Derby Square which earlier in this century was the junction of Preeson's Row.

Preeson's Row was 83 yards in length from Derby Square southward to Redcross Street. The site is now a flagged open space in the vicinity of the city's Law Courts. Although the block was known as Corf's Buildings, it was in fact a street. The term 'buildings' often meant a thoroughfare in 19th-century Liverpool, the most notable being Sir Thomas Buildings, which remains today as Sir Thomas Street. This particular one led from property at the rear of James Street into Redcross Street which once contained court property.

Southerly from James Street at Derby Square before the 1980s stood South Castle Street, now developed into the site of the Queen Elizabeth II Law Courts. Off here stood Cable Street, which is a good example to illustrate the density of drinking dens throughout Victorian Liverpool. Most of the street has now been swallowed up by a bus station. It was formerly 276 yards long and parallel with Lord Street; all that remains of the street beyond the bus station now is an entrance into a car park and a side entrance into the Queen Elizabeth II Law Courts.

During the last century, popular, more well-to-do pubs existed alongside disgusting, unnamed dives where the more 'well off' would drink alongside the working class (similar to their living conditions, where merchants lived in fine houses fronting court property). 25 Cable Street and 30 Lord Street was one such establishment: a nondescript BH until approximately 1850, when named the Palatine. The premises were the headquarters of the Liverpool Chess Club, and claim the distinction of being the first club to play an international game between Liverpool and Calcutta, India, by cable (this had no connection with the name of the street). The moves were telegraphed by a code, presumably invented by one of its members. During the 1880s, the club moved to new premises and for a number of years the old Palatine fell into decay. However, it was rebuilt and renamed the Falcon Restaurant which thrived for many years with the old 'Chess Set' long forgotten. By the 1930s, the premises were listed as the Falcon Club until destroyed during the war. An 1890s Police report states:

'The licensed premises are at the rear of Ruddin Buildings, 30 Lord Street. There are a number of offices in the building, and the occupiers of these have access to the licensed premises from the main entrance to the offices in Lord Street. The licensee does not take any part in the management of the business, he being employed as cashier by the owner at his business, St John's Market.'

Paradise Street was originally named 'Common Shore' after being reclaimed from the site of the old 'pool', rapidly becoming built on after the construction of the old dock. One of its old PHs, listed as 71, was named Man-at-the-Wheel from the days of the old sailing ships: pre-1860s it was named Boatswain's. The pub had a life-sized figure of a 'windjammer helmsman' in bad weather rigout, with the figure's hands holding an actual ship's wheel. The pub was demolished earlier this century.

Listed as 39a Paradise Street was the Star And Garter at the junction with College Lane. It had various uses over the years, including lodging house and hotel at different times. In the 1880s, the premises were listed as Emigration Agents, with the licensed section named the City Vaults. It was probably an 18th-century PH as the premises were mentioned in W. Moss's guide in the 1790s. A car park now occupies this site.

BEEHIVE
Listed as 7 Paradise Street, it is one of two original pubs remaining on the street. It was assumed, at one time, to be a theatre for a short time during the last century. This view of the pub is from before the First World War, when Charles Richardson was licensee. It shows the premises extending out to the right of the photograph. This section has since been demolished and rebuilt and is presently in use as an amusement arcade.

Quinn's Luncheon Bar was listed as 45 Paradise Street at the junction of College Lane. In the 1920s, it was managed by Jimmy Quinn, who subsequently took over the White Star, Rainford Gardens until the 1950s. Previous names for this pub include: Royal Music PH, 1850s; Royal, 1860s-80s; American Saloon, 1890s; then the Alligator until the Second World War. The premises were destroyed during the war and a modern pub. The Trion, was built on the site in the 1960s, now a club named the Escape.

It is known that there was an inn on the site of 17 Paradise Street and 2 School Lane in about 1750. In 1791 a Unitarian Chapel opened here, having moved from Key Street off Tithebarn Street. This remained until 1849, when the premises were sold and converted to a theatre, opening in 1850 as the Royal Colosseum Theatre And Music Hall. From this period until 1904 the theatre changed names and hands on a number of occasions:

1879 Royal Colosseum Temperance Concert Hall
1880 Saunders Theatre Of Varieties
1881 City Theatre Of Varieties

1884 City Theatre And Royal Colosseum
1894 Grand Theatre
1895 New Grand Opera House

In 1878 a real tragedy occurred here. A crowd, assumed to be between four and five thousand, were assembled in the theatre when a minor skirmish erupted in a corner of the pit. The dreaded cry of 'fire' was shouted, causing alarm amongst the audience. With blind panic amongst the throngs of people, the exits became blocked and in a matter of minutes more than thirty people were killed and a large number injured.

In 1904, the old theatre was extensively refurbished as the Queens Theatre having one more name change to Kellys Theatre, before finally closing in the early 1920s. When first opened as a theatre in 1850, in common with others, a pub was attached to the premises. When the new theatre opened, the pub was renamed the Queens Vaults, and remained with the same name after the theatre's

WOODMAN
One of the streets off Canning Place was Mersey Street, now the site of the Merseyside Police Headquarters. Listed as 39, this pub once stood at the junction with Liver Street and was previously called the Woodman And Thatcher Inn.

LYCEUM
Listed as 95, this old pub was situated at the end of Hanover Street at the junction of Brooks Alley. This photograph is from 1912 when the manager was David Williams and shortly before demolition for the construction of an office block that is still standing and known to city centre shoppers as Boots. It was recently taken over by the banking chain T.S.B. The pub and the block were named after the nearby Lyceum Club (recently restored and presently open as a post office). Note the nameplate of Brooks Alley which shows the old spelling 'Brooks's'.

closure; the pub itself closed in the 1930s. A police report from the 1890s states:

> 'At the last annual licensing sessions the licensee gave an undertaking to the Bench not to serve prostitutes: this promise the licensee has failed to carry out, as the police have found prostitutes upon the premises almost nightly. Notice of objection to the renewal of the licence had been served.'

The only pub left on School Lane is the Old Post Office Hotel. The premises were so named about 1800, when a Post Office opened here, before moving to Canning Place in 1839. In the 1890s it was recorded that:

> 'Two workshops on the second floor are reached through one of the entrances, but the stairs are closed with a gate after 6 p.m.'

And, concerning prostitutes:

> 'The management has not been altogether satisfactory, prostitutes having been found on the premises on many occasions, not withstanding the fact that the licensee gave an

undertaking to the Bench at the last annual licensing sessions not to serve this class of women.'

A pub named Dr Syntax was listed as 4 College Lane at the junction of Manestys Lane, off Paradise Street. Described long ago in the 1880s as being an 'old inn', it must have been of ancient age as the structure was that of a low long barn with tiny windows and doors. Its unusual name was apparently adopted in the last century after a well-known race horse of the day. It may well have even been stabled on the premises, as large stables were originally located to the rear. The pub was well known and frequented by its customers for a particular brand of liquor, which had a special, potent beverage named 'Scotch Burgundy', seemingly an old strong ale which had the reputation of having greater healing powers than any other distilled liquor.

One of the former managers of the pub during the 19th century was a Mr Henry Emery, who was once a professional cricketer. The 'All England Eleven Cricket Team' made annual visits to the town and designated the

BALTIC FLEET

The Baltic Fleet is the last pub still standing on Wapping, presently isolated in a triangular site and facing the former Wapping warehouses which have now been converted into luxury apartments. Prior to the demolition of the surrounding property, this pub had three entrances in three different streets: Wapping, Hurst Street and Cornhill Street. Prior to 1972, when the facing docks were fully employed, the pub was frequented by dockers and workers associated with the docks. However, since the closure of the south docks, the pub has closed and reopened on several occasions. Its name is reminiscent of the days of sailing ships, when the cargoes of timber were brought into the adjacent docks from the Baltic area.

RUNCORN VAULTS

Prior to demolition in the 1960s, this large pub was situated at the junction of Wapping and the tiny Runcorn Street which was only 14 yards long. It was listed as 32 Wapping. The photograph is from the 1890s when the manager was Alexander M. Haxfort.

ELLESMERE VAULTS

The Ellesmere Vaults were listed as 1-5 Carpenters Row and 27 Hurst Street, close to Wapping, a typical dockside pub with a number of rooms above it which would have been rented out to the numerous seamen who docked in the town. This pub, along with the Runcorn Vaults, was probably named in connection with the old Duke of Bridgewater's Dukes Dock, which was the distribution point for goods to Runcorn.

OLD POST OFFICE
The only pub left on School Lane is the Old Post Office, although a postal address is 17-19 Old Post Office Place. The premises were so named in approximately 1800, when a Post Office opened here then moved to Canning Place in 1839.

pub as their headquarters. Dr. Syntax finally fell to the bulldozer in the 1930s. A police report from the 1890s states:

'The bar/parlour has been sublet as an outfitter's shop, the entrance to which is through licenses premises. The kitchen is used as a singing room.'

At the junction of Mersey Street was the Custom House Hotel. Another long vanished pub that formerly stood in Canning Place was the Clarence Tavern, at the junction of Litherland Alley. In common with all its neighbouring pubs, it was once a thriving and bustling establishment, when, amongst the din and mayhem of the thirsty customers, frequent voices would be heard spoken in the Welsh tongue. Many Welsh traders would dock in the nearby Canning and Salthouse docks and frequent this pub. A 'club' that regulars once held in this pub is described in the Square Section.

The Canning Place vicinity was the 'centre' of the old sailor town. The quaint alleys of this vicinity were described by E.B. Gerrard in the 1930s:

'Never before in all my wanderings in old Liverpool have I been more quickly transported into the bygone days than when I first stepped from Litherland Alley, near Canning Place, into Ogden Weint. It would not appear that with any stretch of imagination this exceedingly narrow by-way could belong to a modern city. It is so different from any other of our alleys and lanes, and appears to never have been touched by the hand of progress since at least 1650, when the Mersey pushed its way past the bottom of Pool Lane, the present day South Castle Street. Ogden Weint is so narrow that even two pedestrians have difficulty in passing one another without

rubbing shoulders. The large stone flags are very unevenly placed, and at night time when the passage way is dimly illuminated by a flickering yellow light from a gas lamp, one has the feeling of passing down the alleyway of an old sailing ship, and the little doorways, resembling those of ships cabins serve to accentuate the impression.

'Most of the curious lanes of the area are so old that they can count their ages by centuries, and I have no doubt that some of these now rickety buildings were once the homes of comparatively wealthy merchant seamen who chose to live close to their river. Crooked Lane and Litherland Alley, each leading into Ogden Weint, are very similar to one another in many ways. They are both busy centres of forwarding agents, each being a scene of great activity in the day time when creaking cranes are sending down huge bales on to complaining lorries, and the workmen in the warehouse lofts shout and chatter to their co-workers down below. They are both narrow and rutty but well preserved, most of the bricks being, so I am told, hand-made, and the neighbours are proud of them.

'Crooked Lane was always well known to sailors, in fact there was a sea shanty singing the praises of this lane and

KINGS ARMS
A typical, lofty structure so common in the Wapping area. This was formerly listed as 7 Salthouse Lane. An adjoining cocoa rooms is shown on this pre-First World War view. The licensee at the time was Charles A. Hays.

EMPIRE
Opposite Brooks Alley and listed as 70 Hanover Street and 1 Wood Street. It was named in approximately 1914 after reconstruction, prior to this it was named the Dewdrop Inn. The corner door of this view has since been replaced by a window. A police report from 1892 states: 'This house has been most unsatisfactorily conducted during the past year. The police, when visiting, continually find large numbers of prostitutes on the premises. Notice of objection has been served to the renewal of the licence.'

HOUSE OF HANOVER (above)

This large, jaunty pub had three addresses: 28 Canning Place, 2 Hanover Street and 1-3 Price Street. It was previously named Puncheon Tavern and was possibly on the site of the Old Roan. This pub was demolished in the late 1950s for road improvements; its actual site is now landscaped.

BRITISH QUEEN (left)

Argyle Street is one of the narrow streets of the area still standing. The street itself was named after John, Duke of Argyle. The British Queen was a former WSV listed as 15a Argyle Street. Photographed in 1908 where its name is clearly displayed, the licensee at the time was Anthony McDermott.

WSV (above)

Close to Argyle Street is Henry Street, which is another old, narrow street that is still standing. This old WSV once stood at the junction of Henry Street and Suffolk Street. The premises closed in 1906. The manager during the 1890s was Frank Barrow.

ALBERT VAULTS
Before the massive alterations of the area occurred, just a matter of yards from where Price Street led into Canning Place, Frederick Street also ran into Canning Place. This pub stood on the junction of both streets and, like the House of Hanover, had three addresses: 29 Canning Place, 1-3 Frederick Street and 2-4 Price Street.

showing that our "tars" preferred the comforts of Crooked Lane to all the fine foreign countries. The last verse ends like this -

"But I'd rather be in Liverpool
An' listenin' to the rain,
As it rattles on the windows,
In cosy Crooked Lane."'

Sadly, the narrow alleys and lanes mentioned above survived until the 1970s when the bulldozer razed this former quaint area.

From Canning Place in a northeasterly direction is Hanover Street, once called simply the 'high road' where the town's merchants settled as Liverpool's expansion began in the 18th century. In common with most major thoroughfares of the town centre, the merchants eventually moved away as houses, shops and licensed premises gradually took over.

The changes that took place throughout Liverpool are reflected in a list of public houses in Hanover Street over twenty years.

1830s	1850s
1 Burton's Coffee House	Not Listed
2 Old Roan	Not Listed
7 Barrel	Old Barrel
10 Cock	Shropshire Tavern
27 Blue Bell	Surveyor's Office
69 Yorkshire Tavern	Perfumery
Custom House Tavern	Not Listed
Parthenon Tavern	Not Listed
Spread Eagle	Not Listed

During the last century, it was a common occurrence for there to be two separate public houses within the same building between two streets. For example, in the mid-19th century there was the Crewe Hotel on Henry Street (named after the manager during the 1890s, John P. Crewe, and earlier named the Carters Arms) with the Crewe Hotel on Duke Street. The latter was renamed in the 1880s as the Royal Mersey Yacht Hotel and later Royal Yacht.

NEWINGTON HOUSE
Listed as 33-35 Renshaw Street, and located at the junction of Upper Newington. It was photographed in the 1890s with the side of the Shaftesbury Hotel in Upper Newington visible. The manager of the pub during this time was John Galifer. 'Walkers Warrington Ales' is displayed.

86

WHITE HOUSE, Duke Street
This early photograph of the White House from 1908, when the manager was William Gardner, shows the pub had been painted black and white.

The pub closed in the 1960s and apparently had the distinction of being the first pub in Liverpool to acquire a dart board. Adjoining the pub at 92a stood another old pub, the Prince Of Wales, both are presently vacant.

At the corner of Duke Street and Berry Street stands the White House. It was originally a WSV, becoming a PH in about 1874 when the manager, Mr William Townson, only opened the pub six days a week, closing on a Sunday (this was before an Act of Parliament that restricted Sunday hours came into force); the reason being that he had made a promise to his wife never to open on a Sunday. It seemed to have worked

well, for he retired to the comfortable suburban area of Aigburth. The premises then came into the hands of Mr Henry Scott, who completely altered both the interior and exterior of the pub. The outside was painted all white, hence its name. The cost for the alterations was calculated to be £2,000 which was a staggering amount of money during the era.

The following from the *Liverpool Citizen* during the 1880s gives this account concerning the pub's cellar:

'Mr Green, who had recently purchased the premises from Mr Scott, informed me that over £2,000 had been spent on it and after a complete inspection of the premises I could readily have believed that it could have cost much more. I visited the cellars which are exceptionally clean, large and lofty. Mr Green has here introduced a real novelty, which, as far as I am aware, is not to be found in any other house in the city. As it is of great utility, I am sure a brief notice of it will be welcome to all licensed victuallers. Instead of keeping the various descriptions of spirits in store casks ranged in the usual way on shelves near the ceiling of the bar, where the heated atmosphere causes a great deal of evaporation and deteriorate the flavour, Mr Green has his store casks in his cool cellar. The contents of the casks are forced into the pipes connected with the taps in the bar by air pressure, supplied by a small engine. By turning a handle for about five minutes every morning, sufficient air is stored to keep the taps fully supplied throughout the day and the liquor is vastly improved by being kept in this cool spot. I may mention that in front of each store cask is a gauge, which exactly indicates the quality of spirits in the cask, thus saving the necessity of "dipping" with a rod. A glance at

LORD HOWE
Behind the present well-known department store of Lewis's stands Lawton Street. Prior to the 1920s it led through to Renshaw Street and it was at this junction that the pub was located and listed as 2 Renshaw Street and 46 Lawton Street. The pub closed in 1929 and was then demolished, with Lewis's extended over its site.

each tube shows at once if any of the casks require filling up. These two novelties are well worth the attention of the "trade".

In the Berry Street area are two of Liverpool's best-known pubs. Ye Cracke on Rice Street, a narrow thoroughfare off Hope Street, was licensed in approximately 1852, prior to which the premises were part of a block of terraced cottages. Some ten years after opening, the manager acquired an adjoining cottage. Prior to this, although named Ruthin Castle, the premises being so small, it already had the nickname of the Crack which eventually became its name (named Ye Cracke in an 1892 list).

From its early days, it was known as a 'musical snuggery', and the pub was frequented nightly by 'choristers,' in those days only consisting of males, where tenors and bass singers would sing the night away in friendly rivalry. 'Glee Clubs' would often meet here and one of the town's oldest, the Everton Glee Club met here frequently. So popular was this pub with the singing fraternity, they even had their own tipple aptly named a "chorister". Although tucked away down a side street, the pub still attracts musicians today, except the groups now entertain customers, unlike the old Glee Clubs who entertained themselves.

The Philharmonic Hotel at the junction of Hope Street and Hardman Street is the most flamboyant of the large

BLACK HORSE AND RAINBOW
Listed as 21-23 Berry Street, this pub has only been known as such since 1990 and now brews its own ale on the premises. For a short spell prior to this it was named Trader Jacks and before this was for many years known as the Masonic.

ST GEORGE
Listed as 48 Berry Street. This small establishment still trades with very little difference to the exterior from 1904 when the manager was Alfred Peers. The adjoining shop belonged to Alfred Grundy, Tobacconist 46, and 50 was listed to Decimus Wharrie, Chemist.

Edwardian 'gin places' that were built around the turn of the century, although a pub existed earlier on this site. The pub has deservedly won the title 'The most decorative pub in Britain'. It has mosaic floors, stained glass, two smoke rooms named Brahms & Liszt; all contribute to this magnificent pub. Even the gents' toilets are unique, having marble urinals.

An interesting example of a pub changing name can be found on Seel Street at the junction of Back Seel Street. Dr. Duncan's took its name in 1983, after Liverpool's first Medical Officer of Health (and the first in the country). Prior to 1983, it was called the Albert Hotel. A plaque on the side wall in Back Berry Street states:

'Doctor Duncan's - The first Medical Officer of Health, William Henry Duncan, was born at 23 Seel Street in 1805. He was the fifth child of Christian and George Duncan. His mother's family were clerical and came from Dumfriesshire in Scotland. His father's family were Liverpool

OLD WAREHOUSE
Listed as 47 and 1-3 Forrest Street. Pre-1880s it was named the Shropshire Tavern. The photograph is from 1912 when the licensee was William Thompson. The adjoining pub on Park Lane (45) was the Necros Grapes (pre-1880s Sefton Arms), a Threlfalls house managed by John Dudley. The Grapes, shortly after the time of this photograph, was listed as a boarding house.

SV, Park Lane
Formerly listed as 90 Park Lane at the junction with Beckwith Street. This photograph is from the 1920s. Before closure in the 1930s, it was named the Beckwith Vaults, when the manager was William Hoare.

merchants. In those days, Seel Street was in its prime as a residential area. Duncan was forty-two years of age at the time of his appointment as Medical Officer of Health in Liverpool.'

Over one window a plaque reads:

'Doctor William Henry Duncan - Council 11th January 1848: resolved unanimously that William Henry Duncan, Doctor of Medicine, be appointed during the pleasure of the Council, the Medical Officer of Health for the borough of Liverpool at the salary of £750 per annum, it being

understood that he is to give up all private practise and to devote the whole of his time and attention to the duties of the said office.'

Over the other window a plaque reads:

'The 1849 Cholera Epidemic - The epidemic burned itself out by early November 1849 and exactly what impact Duncan's measures had on it is difficult to say. His major contribution to the health of the people of Liverpool was during the ensuing years when, by enforcing the provisions of the Sanitary Act, the standards of housing and environment which created the conditions under which the epidemics could flourish were themselves removed.'

Park Lane, the ancient 'road to Toxteth Park', rapidly became built up after the construction of the town's first dock. As the docks expanded south, new industries and, in particular, dock related businesses such as ship building, ship repairs, sail and rope making, etc., sprang up. Inevitably, the town's slums also grew as this vicinity expanded. During the Second World War, the area of Park Lane took a terrible battering, so much so that the buildings that missed being destroyed were later demolished by city planners. The decade between 1980-90 saw the end of the remaining old pubs on Park Lane.

One of the most prominent of these was the Keans Hotel on the corner of Park Lane and Sparling Street. It is unusual that such a splendid structure had been built on Park Lane when the area at the time would have been a slum district containing much more humble PHs and BHs. The architecture contained an amazing array of design, in particular the roof, which was adorned with urns, balustrades, dolphins, ships, shells and anchors. Researching the history of the pub, I discovered it had evidently been built in error. Plans were made for the railway at Edge Hill to be cut through to Park Lane and a brewery, anticipating the passing trade, had the hotel built on the site of a former SV at the junction of Sparling Street. Only after work had commenced did it come to the attention of the brewers that the proposed station was not for passengers but a goods station. However, it was completed and named the Mayfair Hotel. It was later in use as a public house named the Excelsior and it ended its days as the Keans Hotel.

Another public house in Sparling Street was the Globe, a more typical pub of the area during the 19th century. The view shown in the photograph is from the 1890s where a man and woman are clearly shown in the doorway. Incidentally, the man was wearing clogs - he was probably the licensee, Frederick Zoernack. Written on the door of this pub was the following: 'Si parla italiano - Se habla español - Ici on parle français', indicating that Italian, Spanish and French were spoken here. With the three

KEANS HOTEL
Listed as 172 Park Lane and 2 Sparling Street. This unique hotel was sadly demolished during the 1980s.

THE GLOBE
Listed as 42 Sparling Street off Park Lane. The premises closed in 1910.

countries producing wine, this may have related to a connection with the nearby Wapping Dock where wine was imported, or it may have simply related to visiting seamen from these three countries.

Parallel with Park Lane is Pitt Street, once being a bustling part of Chinatown and a notorious slum area. The Steel Grey Vaults was one of many pubs in the area.

Off Kent Street stands Grenville Street South where, from early in the 19th century until destroyed during the Second World War, stood a pub named the Blue Posts. Pre-1850s this pub was listed as 4 Leveson Street. As a result of one of the most notorious murders in Liverpool, the name Leveson Street was wiped off the map and changed to Grenville Street South. The murder occurred in March 1849, when a Mrs Hinrichson, the wife of a ship's captain, her two children and maid were all brutally murdered by John Gleeson Wilson. Justice was swift during those days for, by the following September, he was executed at Kirkdale Jail.

The continuation of Park Lane southerly is St James Street, as far as the former borough boundary of Parliament Street. Unlike Park Lane, a small number of pubs remain.

During the 19th century the streets west of St James Street, like the streets off Park Lane, were a myriad of squalid slums containing many drinking establishments from the days when numerous sailing ships loaded and discharged in the south docks. Many were gradually cleared from the 1860s and replaced by warehouses that are still abundant in the area today. Most of the pubs in this and the subsequent streets, like the streets nearer the town centre, were mainly demolished by the mid- to late 19th century.

Upper Parliament Street marks the old 'boundary' of the city centre and I have used it as such in this book. In Volume Two, I will look at public houses in the 'outer' city, including Scotland Road, Everton, Dingle and other familiar areas.

CROWN VAULTS
This was listed as 93 Park Lane and 1 Dickinson Street. It was photographed in 1908 when the licensee was Geoffrey Hodgson. Note the early terraced property in Dickinson Street, long since demolished.

WSV
Close to Pitt Street stands Kent Street, which has recently been cleared of its 1930s tenements to be replaced by new housing. This old WSV closed long before the tenements were even built. Formerly listed as 8, it appears the family and the family from the adjoining house were out in force to see the photographer. It was managed by Elizabeth Nelson when photographed in the 1890s, and closed in 1913.

STEEL GREY VAULTS
Note the advert on the window; it seems strange that lager was advertised so long ago. Until the early 1960s, it was rarely consumed (see Introduction). The lager advertised was Amstel, a Dutch brewer who, for many years, were rivals to another Amsterdam brewer, Heineken (the two companies merged in 1968). In March, 1900, the licensee of this pub was fined £5 and costs by the Magistrates for 'being in possession of tobacco mixed with liquor and not enclosed in Customs wrappers.'

CLOCK VAULTS (left)
Listed as 53-55 St James Street and 76 Nelson Street. The facade has changed little in its lifespan of over 80 years. At the other end of Nelson Street, the old property still survives as the heart of Liverpool's Chinatown. The surrounding buildings in this pre-First World War photograph have long gone.

PLOUGH (below)
Formerly listed as 74 St James Street at the junction of Norfolk Street. A sign to the docks is displayed on this 1912 view when the licensee was William R. Tollady: 'Norfolk Street leading to Queens Dock'. Above it is a large advert that displays 'Wine And Spirit Establishment'. A police report from 1892 states: 'Door at Norfolk Street end of entry kept locked at nights'.

FURNACE
Listed as 112 St James Street at the junction with Jordan Street, it almost faced the pub called the Letters. The Furnace closed in 1984 and stood derelict until the premises were demolished in 1989. The area is now landscaped. The photograph shows the pub in the 1920s when the manager was James Suett. Pre-1880s it was listed as St James Vaults. A police report from 1892 states: 'Window of private house in Jordan Street opens into yard of licensed premises. The house was closed in September last, the lease having expired, and reopened in December by the present tenant'.

ROYAL

Listed as 1 Bridgewater Street at the junction of St James Street. Originally it was a WSV before being named. Note the sign on the pub stating 'Bridgewater Street leading to Queens Dock'. The manager was William P. Sutherland when photographed in 1908. The adjoining shop was the English Rabbit Shop. A police report from 1892 states: 'The licensee of this house is a brewer in the employ of the owners of the house, and does not take any part in the management of the business. The licensee of 217 Netherfield Road North manages and resides at this house (Cunard Vaults)'. The pub was acquired by John Smiths Brewery during the 1980s, and a change of business to the shop premises can also be illustrated here. By the 1960s, the shop had become a fruit shop. To date it is a post office, with the pub at the time of writing closed.

THE GRAPES

Listed as 6–8 Bridgewater Street. Pre-1880s it was named Napier Vaults. It closed and was demolished as long ago as 1906, when the premises were replaced by a stable. The photograph is from the 1890s when listed as a 'Beer Retailer' and managed by Thomas Patrick Quinn. Strangely, for a short period during the 1870s, this was listed as the Prince Edward's Island Vaults.

CROWN VAULTS

Listed as 61 Simpson Street and 56 Brick Street, off St James Street. Early in the 19th Century it was named the Blues Tavern, this name being political and not that of an avid Everton fan (Everton F.C. was not in existence at that time). The manger during the 1890s was Francis E. Smith.

GREENLAND ARMS

This dockland street, Greenland Street, got its name from the old whaling ships that once traded in the nearby docks. In common with other streets of the area, this street once contained many pubs. This one was listed as 2 Greenland Street and 140 St James Street. Another common feature is the nameplate indicating Queens Dock. This was the last pub on the street in the 1970s and has now been replaced by landscaping. It was photographed in 1912 when the licensee was Thomas Greetham. It had the earlier name of the Grapes and, pre-1860s, Hope Tavern.

BELFRY

Listed as 35 St James Road. During the 1980s, St James Road was physically 'cut up' from its old line as part of the new housing and landscaping scheme outside the Cathedral. This pub, formerly named the Nelson, stood at the junction of Nile Street and was demolished in the 1970s. The photograph is from the 1920s when the manageress was Mrs Clara Vester.

GREAT GEORGE HOTEL

This was located as 68 Upper Pitt Street and was open during the 1820s when it was named the St George's Tavern and listed as 29. A well-known tavern of the last century that boasted its own chess and cricket club, it was a noted political house. During the last century, it was for many years the headquarters of the local 'Tory Party'. It was from an upstairs window on the premises that the Right Honourable William Ewart Gladstone delivered one of his earliest speeches. It remained open until the 1960s. This photograph is from 1908 when the licensee was Percy Williams.

ACKNOWLEDGEMENTS

I would like to thank the following for their help with research and material:

Bass Taverns and Maria Murray of Bar One Eleven.

Colin Wilkinson, Sarah Jennings & Lisa Jackson, Bluecoat Press.

Janet Smith & Staff, Central Library, Liverpool.

Staff, Crosby Library.

Roger Hull, Southport Library.

Lancashire Records Office.

Ian Green & Staff, Reprographics Dept., Liverpool City Council.

Community Services Dept., Merseyside Police.

Margaret Proctor & Staff, Record Office.

Joanne Davison, Licensing Section.

Zena Taylor, Eileen Turton & Staff at Peter Walker, Duke Street Office, Liverpool.

The following I would like to thank for their personal contributions:

Harold Andrus

Marie McQuade

Peter Scott

Ted Williams

Ronnie E. Brown

Geoff Roberts

Bobby Shack

Special thanks to my wife Jean, my Dad and brother Frank

Last but not least a special thank you to John McKeown, without whose dedication and research this book would not be possible.

Also a mention for my fellow members of the Whingeing Winos Club of Yates Wine Lodge in Manchester Street (especially Tommy Williams who frequented the premises practically every day from 1945 until closure).

Scroll holders: John E. Puddifer, Tommy Beverage, Tommy Williams, Freddie Nutbrown, Henry Foy, Sean Quinn (Manager), Tommy Lavery, Stan Lewis, John Peter Lloyd, James Alfred Wright, Joseph Burns, Freddy O'Connor, Dominic Whelan, John Higham, Bryn Jones, Hugh Venables, George Williams, Jerry McLean, Kenneth Edward Pennington, Eddie Ormesher, Pat Edwards, Sheila Edwards, Richard Kevin Walsh, Vinny Hughes, Robert William Knowles, Peter Flynn, Derek Flynn, George Cain, Ronnie Wheetman, Tommy Pomeroy. Other members: Franny Armstrong, Peter Armstrong, Joey Armstrong, Derek Bedford, Bob Bird, Eddie Blackhall, Peter (Pop) Brennan, Jimmy Brown, Joe Brown, Joe Burns, Albert Campbell, Jackie Campbell, Mick Campbell, Ronnie Challinor, Terry Clarke, Brian (Gazza) Cook, Bernard Davies, Brian Dawson, Johnny Deane (former resident singer), Tony Devitt, Frank Dunne, Jimmy Dunne, Dave Edwards, Ernie Laycock, Joe Lindsey, John Lyness, Frank (Franno) McAllister, Dennis McCann, Jimmy McCabe, Francis McGrath, Terry McKane, Vicky McKane, Paul McShana, John McVey, Tony Macrin, Danny Marlow, John & Peter (twins) Mason, Arthur Mitchell, Richie Mulvey, John Nesbitt, Denny Nicholls, Jimmy Nolan, Jimmy O'Dowd, Ray (Twig) Ormesher, Sid Ormesher, Richie Owens, John Edwards, Tommy Feeney, Terry Fisher, Tommy (Golly) Gallagher, Jimmy (Gibbo) Giblin, Tony Gilboy, Terry Gilligan, Terry Glennen, John Gorman, Harry Graham, Norman Green, Bob Grice, Alan Howard, John Howard, George Jackson, Robert Jones, Brian Keegan, Justin Kehoe, Dennis John Kelly, John Kerwin, Ronnie Knibb, Chris (Christie) Knowles, Franny Porter, Harold Prytherch, George Quinn, John Rimmer, Gerry Roach, Paul Rodney, Tommy Ryan, John Shea, Ted (Stevo) Stephens, Ronnie Swaine, Ted Thomas, Peter Tierney, Peter Tootle, (Big Eddie) Vale, Tim (U.S.A.) Wallace, Ronnie Whittaker, Tommy Williams, George Winstanley, Gerry Woods.